At Issue

Are Americans Overmedicated?

Other Books in the At Issue Series:

At Issue

Are Americans Overmedicated?

Tamara Thompson, Book Editor

GREENHAVEN PRESS
A part of Gale, Cengage Learning

GALE
CENGAGE Learning

Detroit • New York • San Francisco • New Haven, Conn • Waterville, Maine • London

Christine Nasso, *Publisher*
Elizabeth Des Chenes, *Managing Editor*

© 2011 Greenhaven Press, a part of Gale, Cengage Learning.

Gale and Greenhaven Press are registered trademarks used herein under license.

For more information, contact:
Greenhaven Press
27500 Drake Rd.
Farmington Hills, MI 48331-3535
Or you can visit our Internet site at gale.cengage.com

For product information and technology assistance, contact us at

Gale Customer Support, 1-800-877-4253
For permission to use material from this text or product, submit all requests online at www.cengage.com/permissions

Further permissions questions can be emailed to permissionrequest@cengage.com

Articles in Greenhaven Press anthologies are often edited for length to meet page require-ments. In addition, original titles of these works are changed to clearly present the main thesis and to explicitly indicate the author's opinion. Every effort is made to ensure that Greenhaven Press accurately reflects the original intent of the authors. Every effort has been made to trace the owners of copyrighted material.

Cover Image copyright © Images.com/Corbis.

LIBRARY OF CONGRESS CATALOGING-IN-PUBLICATION DATA

Are Americans overmedicated? / Tamara Thompson, book editor.
    p. cm. -- (At issue)
Includes bibliographical references and index.
ISBN 978-0-7377-5141-3 (hardcover) -- ISBN 978-0-7377-5142-0 (pbk.)
1. Americans--Drug use. 2. Drug utilization--United States. I. Thompson, Tamara.
RM138.A74 2011
615'.10973--dc22

                                         2010038102

Contents

Introduction

When most people think about drug use in America, they think about illegal drugs such as marijuana or cocaine. But pharmaceuticals are far more widely used than illicit drugs are, and the use of such medications has skyrocketed over the past two decades. According to a 2006 study by Boston University, 82 percent of American adults and more than half of children now take at least one medication (prescription or nonprescription drugs, vitamins or herbal supplements) every day. Nearly 30 percent of adults take five or more daily; 27 percent of children take two or more. Americans fill more than 3.5 billion prescriptions from their doctors each year, accounting for nearly half of the global pharmaceutical market.

Americans are, without question, the most heavily medicated people on the planet. But regardless of whether that illustrates a penchant for quick fixes and overly permissive prescribing—as some critics say—or whether it reflects better health screening and more accessible treatments—as the drug industry says—the forces that shape the statistics are themselves highly controversial.

The main force is the pharmaceutical industry. With $291 billion in annual sales, the pharmaceutical industry is the fastest-growing and most profitable sector of the US economy, and spending on prescription drugs is the fastest-growing category of health-care expense.

According to the nonpartisan Center for Public Integrity, the pharmaceutical industry spent $855 million—more than any other industry—on lobbying from 1998 to 2006. In 2009 the industry had 1,228 lobbyists, more than 2 for every member of Congress. Whether related to drug safety oversight, Medicare prescription coverage, or the drug-patent extension in President Barack Obama's health-care reform package (approved by the Senate in March 2010), all such lobbying is intended to translate into public policies that favor profits for pharmaceutical companies, often known collectively as Big Pharma.

Besides lawmakers, a critical focus for Big Pharma's influence is the Food and Drug Administration (FDA), the government agency responsible for regulating the testing, manufacturing, labeling, advertising, marketing, efficacy, and safety of prescription drugs in the United States. A large part of the FDA's funding comes from fees paid by pharmaceutical companies as their drugs move through the regulatory process. Many critics argue that this practice is akin to letting the fox guard the henhouse because the agency is charged with scrutinizing the products of the very people that are paying its bills. Because of its close ties to drug companies the FDA has been highly criticized in recent years for acting more like a partner of the industry than its watchdog.

Besides seeking to influence policy makers and government agencies, Big Pharma spends $3 billion a year marketing drugs directly to consumers, and another $15 billion a year marketing to doctors, who they hope will prescribe their products. While drug makers say they are simply striving to educate both the public and physicians about the benefits of their medications, critics say the real purpose and obvious result is to drive sales of drugs that may not be necessary or appropriate for an individual. Physicians are indeed increasingly likely to write prescriptions—if not because they have been influenced by drug companies, then because health insurers, including the government's Medicare program for seniors, typically cover the cost of medications, but not that of nondrug therapies that can be equally effective but often more expensive.

A good example is the antidepressant Prozac, which was quickly seen as a cost-effective replacement for psychotherapy when it was introduced to treat depression in 1988. Within five years, 4.5 million Americans had taken Prozac, and annual US sales topped out at $2.7 billion before the drug's patent expired in 2001. Prozac was the first mass-marketed "blockbuster" drug, and it reinvented the way medicines are prescribed, sold and promoted in the United States. It also reinvented the way Americans perceive mental health issues by mainstreaming treatment and ushering in a new era of popularized medications for depression and other mental disorders.

Aside from Big Pharma's massive marketing machine and an American culture primed to embrace its message, the number of people taking psychiatric drugs grew further because the *Diagnostic and Statistical Manual of Mental Disorders* (DSM-IV), the official criteria manual used to diagnose psychiatric disorders—broadened its criteria for many conditions. More easily met criteria meant more people could be diagnosed with a disorder and receive medication. As an example, when the criteria for attention-deficit/hyperactivity disorder (ADHD) was broadened, critics allege, many healthy but very active children easily met the threshold for diagnosis. Sales of ADHD drugs jumped nearly 500 percent in just a decade. By 2004 some 2.5 million American children were taking ADHD drugs, including almost 10 percent of ten-year-old boys nationwide.

According to Big Pharma's critics, another reason medication use has increased is that pharmaceutical companies have literally invented new diseases for their pills to treat. An example of such a practice is the drug Detrol for "overactive bladder," a condition that did not exist until the drug maker coined the term and then spent millions teaching doctors how to recognize it. Detrol has since turned into a blockbuster drug, with annual sales of $1.2 billion. "We are taking too many drugs for dubious or exaggerated ailments," says physician Marcia Angell, former editor of the *New England Journal of Medicine*. "What the drug companies are doing now is promoting drugs for long-term use to essentially healthy people. Why? Because it is the biggest market."

Drug makers, however, explain their stellar sales growth by saying it is a matter of better treatment options. "We now have more medicines and better medicines for more diseases," says Jeff Trewhitt, a spokesman for the Pharmaceutical Research and Manufacturers of America (PhRMA), a trade organization that represents the country's leading pharmaceutical and biotechnology companies.

Whether such heavy and widespread medication use is appropriate or whether Americans are overmedicated is an ongoing controversy, but a growing number of doctors, researchers, and public health experts believe that, whatever the case, the pharmaceutical industry must be reformed. In her book *Our Daily Meds*, Melody Petersen, a former pharmaceutical industry reporter for the *New York Times*, sets forth a plan to do just that. Among her ideas:

- A law should be enacted that prohibits doctors from accepting money or gifts from pharmaceutical companies, which likewise should be prohibited from giving them.

- The government should establish an independent agency to keep the research interests of science and the public good separate from the profit-driven motives of pharmaceutical companies.

- To undo a deeply entrenched conflict of interest, the FDA should no longer be supported by fees paid by pharmaceutical companies.

- Because under-the-radar promotion is far more powerful than direct advertising, practices such as using celebrity spokespeople, having sales reps promote medicines directly to doctors, and letting drug companies sponsor public events, disease screenings, and physician education should be banned.

Whether implementing any or all of these suggestions would alter the number of pills Americans take is unclear, but many believe that reforming the industry's practices would be an important first step toward reducing the undue influence of drug companies and bolstering consumer protection. The authors in *At Issue: Are Americans Overmedicated?* represent a wide range of viewpoints concerning the consumption of pharmaceutical drugs and the forces that shape their widespread use and cultural acceptance.

1

Americans Take Too Many Prescription Drugs

J. Douglas Bremner

J. Douglas Bremner is a physician and researcher who publishes the popular drug and health safety blog Before You Take That Pill.

Americans take more prescription medications than any other people in the world, and it is mostly because of the power and influence of pharmaceutical companies. Government deregulation and the weakening of the Food and Drug Administration (FDA) in the 1980s allowed new drugs to be approved with greater speed and less scrutiny than before; then, in 1992, fees collected from drug companies became the major source of funding for the FDA. This conflict of interest continues today, and Big Pharma's deep influence means that the FDA's decisions usually favor the profit-driven interests of the pharmaceutical industry rather than protecting consumers. The drug industry is a major marketing machine that spends more money to convince people they need drugs—and to convince doctors to prescribe them—than it does to create the drugs themselves.

The latest drive to get new pills on the shelves and into people's mouths began when government deregulation and an earnest attempt to help AIDS-HIV patients access important life-extending drugs collided. In the 1980s there was a

J. Douglas Bremner, *Before You Take That Pill: Why the Drug Industry May Be Bad for Your Health: Risks and Side Effects You Won't Find on the Labels of Commonly Prescribed Drugs, Vitamins, and Supplements.* New York: Avery, 2008. Copyright © 2008. All rights reserved. Reproduced by permission.

strong movement to decrease the role of government regulation in all businesses, and budgets of regulatory agencies like the FDA [Food and Drug Administration] were slashed as part of that effort. The [Ronald] Reagan Administration painted the FDA as a bloated bureaucracy that was slowing down the approval of drugs and getting in the way of business.

There was some truth to that claim. At that time it could take up to two years to gain drug approval, two years too long if you were suffering from HIV-AIDS. Throughout the 1980s, AIDS activists and patients echoed the drug companies' sentiments, complaining that it took too long to bring disease-fighting drugs to market. The pharmaceutical industry lent a sympathetic ear and a loud voice to calls for speed in approvals of AIDS drugs such as Agenerase (amprenavir). Since drugs are on patent for a limited number of years, every year spent waiting for approval from the FDA meant losing a year of profits.

Couple that with the fact that the FDA could now honestly say that, because of cuts, it was understaffed. The answer was essentially legislation allowing pharmaceutical companies to pay the salaries of the staff at the FDA. In 1992, the Prescription Drug User Fee Act (PDUFA) stipulated that a fee (now $576,000) be paid to the FDA by the pharmaceutical companies for each new drug application. The number of staff at the Center for Drug Evaluation and Research (CDER) doubled overnight. Today, the FDA receives about $260 million a year from these fees. Part of the bill stipulated that funding by Congress for new drug evaluations had to increase by 3% per year. Since the overall funding for the FDA did not increase at 3% per year, the FDA had to actually cut funding for surveillance and research of approved drugs.

Conflicts of Interest

Another interesting phenomenon resulted from the change in law: the boundaries between the drug companies, FDA, and doctors became increasingly blurred. FDA officials sometimes move to jobs in the pharmaceutical industry, which means they may not want to burn their bridges with industry. The same FDA officials who approve the drugs are responsible for monitoring them after they are on the market, which gives them an obvious disincentive to say that the drugs they earlier certified as safe were now unsafe. Finally, the FDA gets input from outside advisory panels made up of doctors who are experts in their fields. Most of these doctors receive payments as consultants, research grants and support for travel to conferences from drug companies. In some cases, the doctors are working as paid consultants to the same companies whose drugs are coming up for approval by their advisory committees.

For instance, as reported by *USA Today* on October 16, 2004 ("Cholesterol Guidelines Become a Morality Play") eight of the nine doctors who formed a committee in 2001 to advise the government on cholesterol guidelines for the public were making money from the very same companies that made the cholesterol-lowering drugs that they were urging millions of Americans to take. For example, one of the committee members, Dr. H. Bryan Brewer, was the Chief of the Molecular Disease Branch at the National Institutes of Health [NIH]. He worked as a consultant or speaker for 10 different pharmaceutical companies, making over $100,000 over three years while he was on the committee, and sat on one of their boards (*Los Angeles Times*, December 22, 2004, "The National Institutes of Health: Public Servant or Private Marketer?"). Dr. Brewer left the NIH in 2005 in the midst of adverse publicity about potential conflicts of interest. Nassir Ghaemi, MD, a psychiatrist at Emory University, was quoted in the *Emory Academic Exchange* (February, 2007) as saying, "Critics say we are being influenced and don't realize it—that drug companies are smarter than we are and know a lot more about human psychology than we think, and they're probably right about that to some extent."

Increasing Pressure to Prescribe

Expert consensus guidelines have a potent effect on doctors; they can be held liable if they do not adhere to accepted standards of care. Dr. Curt D. Furberg, a former head of clinical trials at the National Heart, Lung, and Blood Institute and now a professor at Wake Forest University in North Carolina, explained how such information reached physicians: "The [company] reps tell the doctors, 'You should follow these guidelines,' implying that you're not a good doctor if you don't follow these guidelines." (*Los Angeles Times*, December 22, 2004, "The National Institutes of Health: Public Servant or Private Marketer?)"

To gain the most market share, companies have to invent drugs for diseases that previously had no treatment . . . or create prevention medications for alleged risks.

The result of this co-mingling was a boon for drug makers, approval time of their products decreased from 20 months to six months right after the law changed. However, the number of drugs that had to be later withdrawn also increased from 2% of drugs to 5% of drugs.

There is another troubling dichotomy that could have terrible repercussions for our health: while the number of people with disease is not growing, the number of adult Americans taking medication is increasing—half of us take prescription drugs and 81% of us take at least one kind of pill everyday—and that percentage is expected to rise in the coming years. To gain the most market share, companies have to invent drugs for diseases that previously had no treatment (or treat problems that may not necessarily require drug treatment, such as "restless leg syndrome"), or create prevention medications for alleged risks (like the risk of fracture in the elderly) by expanding the potential pool of medication takers. That meant moving from the realm of giving medications to sick people, to giving medications to people who looked well, but might be at an increased risk based on the result of a blood test or some other hidden marker of disease. Thus the era of disease prevention and risk factor modification was born.

The US is the only country in the world where you can turn on the TV and have an announcer tell you to go 'ask your doctor' for a drug.

To promote this shift, for the past two decades the pharmaceutical industry has pushed educational programs, which they claim are designed to identify people in need of treatment or prevention with medication. This is usually done by donating money to organizations who advocate on behalf of a specific disease who will in turn "get the word out," increasing public awareness and screening, and expanding the number of individuals who will potentially take the medication. This is fine for identifying individuals with undiagnosed high blood pressure or to detect the early stages of colon cancer. But awareness campaigns are not always meant to be purely, altruistically educational. Most are linked to a drug company's marketing campaign.

Benefits Questioned

There are a number of conditions for which we are now urged to obtain screening and potential treatment, including high cholesterol, osteoporosis, hypertension, diabetes, and undetected heart disease. However, the potential benefit of medications to treat these conditions is often exaggerated, side effects are minimized, and in some cases recommendations are applied to people based on evidence from different groups of people (e.g. women with risk factors for heart disease are urged to take cholesterol-lowering medications based on studies in men). In addition, doctors who work as paid consultants to the pharmaceutical industry often write the guidelines about who should take the drugs, so it is unclear how unbiased their recommendations really are.

Another factor that has expanded use of prescription medications happened in 1997, when the FDA lifted the ban on direct to consumer advertising along with the law that required ads to list every possible side effect. Soon after, Americans were bombarded daily with commercials for prescription drugs. The US is the only country in the world where you can turn on the TV and have an announcer tell you to go 'ask your doctor' for a drug. Doctors often will give medications to patients even if they don't think they need it. For example, one study showed that 54% of the time doctors will prescribe a specific brand and type of medication if patients ask for it.

A Bleak Diagnosis

With so many of us popping pills or gulping down spoonfuls of medicine, it's not surprising that more of us report related adverse effects. One hundred thousand Americans die every year from the effects of prescription medications. Over a million Americans a year are admitted to the hospital because they have had a bad reaction to a medication. About a quarter of the prescriptions that doctors write for the elderly have a potentially life threatening error. Many of these people are getting medications that they don't need, or for problems that can be appropriately and safely addressed without drugs. For example, most cases of adult onset diabetes can be prevented and possibly cured with a change in diet alone—and with considerably fewer negative side effects and numerous healthy ones, like weight loss, and lower blood pressure and cholesterol. . . .

Drugs Do Not Improve Outcomes

I'm not saying that some drugs don't ever successfully prevent disease, or that newly described diseases and syndromes are necessarily invalid. But the fact is that no matter how you look at it, the US (and to a lesser extent other countries) has a prescription drug problem. The US spends two times more on drugs, and takes twice as many drugs, as other countries, and has worse health. That means we are paying money for drugs that are not working for us.

It is time for Americans to rethink the role of medications and other pills in their lives in relation to other actions that can be taken to maximize health.

Despite the fact that Americans spend twice as much on health care as any other country in the world, we have some of the worst healthcare outcomes in the industrialized world, including total life expectancy, and survival of children to their 5th birthday. In a survey of 13 industrialized nations, the US was found to be last in many health-related measures, and overall was 2nd to the last. Countries with the best health care included Japan, Sweden, and Canada, in that order. Factors that were thought to explain worse healthcare outcomes in the US included the lack of a developed and effective primary care system and higher rates of poverty. Even England, which has higher rates of smoking and drinking and a fattier diet, has better health than the US. . . .

It is time for Americans to rethink the role of medications and other pills in their lives in relation to other actions that can be taken to maximize health, such as making changes in diet; incorporating exercise into one's daily routine; learning and using stress reduction techniques; and changing other behaviors like quitting smoking. The most common disorders, like diabetes and heart disease, are always better treated and prevented through changes in diet, exercise, and lifestyle than they are with medication. Pharmaceuticals can be life saving for some conditions, such as insulin for Type I diabetes, thyroid hormone for hypothyroidism, or antibiotics for life threatening infections. All of this has been shown through several scientific studies. Before you take that pill, consider taking charge of your health by making informed decisions and smart changes in your lifestyle. In some cases, however, you may need medications for prevention or treatment of disease, or to help you with troubling symptoms or disabilities. In those cases you should know as much as you can about the risks and benefits, so that when it is time to talk to your doctor you can make an informed decision that both of you are happy with.

2

Prescription Drugs Help
Millions Live Better Lives

Pharmaceutical Researchers and Manufacturers of America (PhRMA)

The Pharmaceutical Researchers and Manufacturers of America (PhRMA) is a lobbying organization that represents the country's leading pharmaceutical research and biotechnology companies.

Advances in medical science have led to important medications that help people live longer and healthier lives. Drugs for HIV have drastically reduced the death rate from AIDS; cholesterol-lowering statin drugs have reduced the need for invasive heart surgeries; blood-thinning drugs help prevent devastating strokes; diabetes medicines help people avoid serious complications from that disease; and anticancer drugs have increased cancer survivor rates and added 10.7 percent to life expectancy at birth for Americans. Because medicines can prevent or manage diseases, overall health-care costs are lower as people do not need as many expensive treatments, hospitalization, or surgeries. Medicines also benefit the economy because people lose fewer days of work and are more productive when they take medications for their health problems. The pharmaceutical industry also contributes to economic stability by creating thousands of jobs ranging from sales representatives to scientific researchers.

Over the last few decades, scientists have made substantial progress in the discovery of new medicines. Even more dramatic advances are anticipated in the years ahead through research in new fields such as genomics and proteomics.

In the last decade alone, over 300 new medicines have been approved by the FDA [Food and Drug Administration]. These advances are improving the treatment of common diseases like heart disease, diabetes, and cancer, as well as rare disorders like Fabry's disease, cystic fibrosis, and sickle cell anemia.

As a result of these new discoveries, medicines are taking on an increasingly important role in patient care. As a result, we are spending more on pharmaceuticals. In return, more patients are living longer, better lives; overall health care costs are restrained as patients avoid invasive surgeries and costly hospital and nursing home stays; and the economy is strengthened through improved worker productivity.

Studies Confirm Value of Medicines

A growing number of studies are confirming the increasing value of new medicines to patients and society. For example, a study by Frank R. Lichtenberg, the Courtney C. Brown Professor of Business at Columbia University, finds that patients using newer drugs were significantly less likely to die and lose workdays than those using older drugs. Lichtenberg also found that the use of newer medicines increased drug costs by $18, but reduced hospital and other non-drug costs by $129,[1] meaning that for each additional $1 spent on newer pharmaceuticals, $6.17 is saved in total health care spending, $4.44 of which comes from savings in hospital spending.

New Medicines Save and Improve Lives

- New medicines have made a major contribution to the decline in the death rate from HIV/AIDS in the U.S. over the last 10 years. Since the mid-1990s, when researchers developed a new wave of medicines to treat HIV/AIDS, the U.S. death rate from AIDS dropped about 70%.[2]

- Several studies have found that use of statin therapy to treat people with high cholesterol reduces hospital admissions and invasive cardiac surgeries. For example, a study of one statin showed that it reduced hospital admissions by a third during five years of treatment. It also reduced the number of days that patients had to spend in the hospital when they were admitted, and reduced the need for bypass surgery and angioplasty.[3]

- A study sponsored by the Agency for Health Care Policy and Research concluded that increased use of a blood-thinning drug would prevent 40,000 strokes a year, saving $600 million annually.[4]

- A February 2004 study by Lichtenberg finds that new cancer drugs have accounted for 50% to 60% of the gains we have made in cancer survival rates since 1975. Since 1971, when the U.S. declared war on cancer, our arsenal of cancer medicines has tripled. During that time, the survival rate rose from 50% to 67%. Overall, new cancer drugs have contributed a remarkable 10.7% of the increase in life expectancy at birth in the U.S.[5]

New Medicines Help Control Health Care Costs

- A January 2004 study by Duke [University] researchers found that "beta-blocker therapy improves the clinical outcomes of heart failure patients and is cost saving to society and Medicare." The study, which was written before enactment of the Medicare drug benefit, notes: "If medication costs were completely reimbursed by Medicare, program savings from beta-blocker therapy would remain positive."[6] Looking at the overall societal perspective, the researchers found that five years of treatment for heart failure without beta-blockers cost a total of $52,999. With beta-blockers added to treatment, total treatment costs fell by $3,959, patient survival increased by an average of about three-and-a-half months, and patients needed fewer overnight hospital stays.

- New studies are showing how newer, better medicines reduce the cost of treating people with depression. The cost of treating a depressed person fell throughout the 1990s, "largely because of a switch from hospitalization to medication," the *Wall Street Journal* said in a December 31, 2003 story on the study. The study, published in the *Journal of Clinical Psychiatry* in December 2003, found that per-patient spending on depression fell by 19% over the course of the decade.[7]

- New diabetes medicines are helping patients avoid serious complications and death, and can reduce overall health care spending. One recent study found that effective treatment of diabetes with medicines and other therapy yields annual health care savings of $685–$950 per patient within one to two years.[8] Another study corroborated these results, finding that use of a disease management program to control diabetes with medicines and patient education generated savings of $747 per patient per year.[9]

- A study of the effects of a new Alzheimer's medicine, donepezil, on costs in a Medicare managed care plan showed that, although the prescription costs for the group receiving the drug were over $1,000 higher per patient, the overall medical costs fell to $8,056 compared with $11,947 for the group not receiving drug treatment. This one-third savings was the result of reduced costs in other areas, such as hospital and skilled nursing facility costs.[10]

New Medicines Strengthen the Economy

- America's pharmaceutical companies create thousands of high-quality, U.S.-based jobs. In addition to employing over 70,000 scientists, the pharmaceutical research industry directly employs more than 315,000 Americans.[11]

- New medicines also benefit the economy by increasing worker productivity and reducing absenteeism. One study, which evaluated the effect of migraine treatment on productivity, found that more than 50% of workers who received a triptan drug injection for a migraine attack returned to work within two hours, compared with 9% of workers who received a placebo.[12]

- A study in the *Journal of Occupational and Environmental Medicine* found that patients taking a non-sedating antihistamine for allergies experienced a 5.2% increase in daily work output in the three days after receiving the medication, compared with a 7.8% reduction in work output for workers receiving sedating antihistamines.[13]

- The National Committee for Quality Assurance (NCQA) says that "if every American with depression received care from a health plan or provider that was performing at the 90th percentile level, employers would recover up to 8.8 million absentee days a year."[14] NCQA also reported that only 40.1% of patients with depression "received effective continuation phase treatment."

Notes

1. Frank R. Lichtenberg, *"Benefits and Costs of Newer Drugs: An Update,"* (Cambridge, MA: National Bureau of Economic Research, June 2002).

2. CASCADE Collaboration, *"Determinants of Survival Following HIV-1 seroconversion after introduction of HAART,"* The Lancet, 362 (2003): 1267–1274.

3. *"Cholesterol Pill Linked to Lower Hospital Costs,"* The New York Times, 27 March, 1995.

4. D.B Matchar, G.P. Samsa, *Secondary and Tertiary Prevention of Stroke, Patient Outcomes Research Team (PORT) Final Report—Phase 1,* AHRQ Pub. No. 00–N001, Rockville, MD: Agency for Healthcare Research and Quality, June 2000.

5. Frank R. Lichtenberg, *"The Expanding Pharmaceutical Arsenal in the War on Cancer,"* National Bureau of Economic Research Working Paper No. 10328 (Cambridge, MA: NBER, February 2004).

6. PA Cowper, et al., *"Economic Effects of Beta-Blocker Therapy in Patients with Heart Failure,"* The American Journal of Medicine, 116 (2004): 2 104–111.

7. PE Greenberg, et al., *"The Economic Burden of Depression in the United States: How Did It Change Between 1990 and 2000?"* Journal of Clinical Psychiatry, 64 (2003): 1465–1475.

8. E.H. Wagner, et al., *"Effect of Improved Glycemic Control on Health Care Costs and Utilization,"* Journal of the American Medical Association, 285 (2001): 2, 182–189.

9. J. Berger, et al., *"Economic Impact of a Diabetes Disease Management Program in a Self-Insured Heath Plan: Early Results,"* Disease Management, 4 (2001): 2, 65–73.

10. JW Hill, et al., *"The Effect of Donepezil Therapy on Health Costs in a Managed Care Plan,"* Managed Care Interface, (March 2002): 63–70.

11. National Science Foundation, Division of Science Resources Statistics, Survey of Industrial Research and Development: 200 (Arlington, VA: NSF, 2000).

12. R.C. Cady, et al., *"Sumatriptan Injection Reduces Productivity Loss During a Migraine Attack: Results of a Double-Blind, Placebo-Controlled Trial,"* Archives of Internal Medicine, 158 (11 May 1998.)

13. I.M. Cockburn, et al., *"Loss of Work Productivity Due to Illness and Medical Treatment,"* Journal of Occupational and Environmental Medicine, 41 (1999): 11, 948–953.

14. National Committee for Quality Assurance, State of Health Care Quality: 2002 (Washington, DC: NCQA, 2003).

3

Psychiatric Drugs Are Overprescribed

Charles Barber

Charles Barber is a lecturer in psychiatry at the Yale University School of Medicine and a senior executive at The Connection, a nonprofit social services agency in Connecticut.

The widespread use of antidepressants has changed the American psyche in deeper ways than those caused by the action of drugs in people's brains. As mainstream use of psychiatric drugs has grown more commonplace over the past two decades, mental illness and psychiatry have become everyday topics of conversation—and of popular entertainment. Because of such widespread acceptance, instead of treating the severe mental health issues for which they were invented, antidepressants are now overwhelmingly prescribed for the simple stresses and anxieties of everyday life. Americans spent more than $13.5 billion on antidepressants in 2006, and the psychiatric drug industry has become one of the most powerful industries in the world. Most of the people taking these drugs do not really need them, however. Americans are the most psychiatrically medicated people in the world, and unnecessarily so.

The size and reach of the psychiatric drug industry is staggering. It is far, far greater than most psychiatric practitioners realize and certainly greater than the drug companies would want you to know. There are various ways to measure the dimensions of the enterprise:

- 33 million Americans were prescribed at least one psychiatric drug in 2004, up from 21 million in 1997.

- The spending on antidepressants rose from $5.1 billion in 1997 to $13.5 billion in 2006; and on antipsychotics from $1.3 billion in 1997 to 11.5 billion in 2006.

- The third-best-selling antidepressant, Lexapro, has been on the market only since 2002. But 15 million Americans have already taken it.

- Nine percent of American teens have been prescribed drugs for depression.

- The products are not limited to adults, and not even to humans. In 2002, 11 million antidepressant prescriptions were written for American children and adolescents. Before 1990, outside of the occasional use of Ritalin, the medicating of kids was just about taboo. Clomicalm (known as Anafranil when taken by humans) is approved by the FDA [Food and Drug Administration] for separation anxiety for dogs. To increase their appeal for these segments of the market, Prozac and Paxil come in mint- and orange-flavored liquids, respectively, and Clomicalm is meat-flavored. A Los Angeles veterinarian estimates that 5 percent of the cats and dogs in his practice are taking psychotropic agents for their behavior.

- Zoloft's American sales—$3.1 billion in 2005—exceeded those of Tide detergent that same year.

- The worldwide sales of one drug for schizophrenia, Zyprexa—$4.7 billion in 2006—were greater than the revenue generated by the [clothing maker] Levi Strauss Co.

A Shift in Attitudes

Accompanying the sales of the drugs (indeed what has made the sales and ingestion of the drugs possible, at least in part) has been an equally dramatic attitude shift toward mental dysfunction on the part of Americans. As the drugs have sailed to the top of the charts, mental illness and psychiatry have gone from being taboo subjects to becoming almost chic.

Madness has . . . become alluring and inviting and, at the very least, enormously popular.

[TV mobster] Tony Soprano takes Prozac, lithium, and Xanax (and his mother, Livia, took Prozac, and AJ, his son, is put on Lexapro, a newer antidepressant, in the show's last season.) [TV psychologist] Dr. Phil is a star. [Rapper] Eminem is on antidepressants. [Actresses] Lorraine Bracco (who happens to play Tony Soprano's psychiatrist) and Halle Berry suffer from depression; [Actress and model] Brooke Shields, from postpartum depression; and [soccer star] David Beckham, from obsessive-compulsive disorder. Hardly a week goes by without a celebrity revealing—usually in some well-chosen commercial format—their long-secret psychiatric disorder. . . .

Behavior as Biology

To further the ascent of Prozac et al. it has helped immensely that there has been a simultaneous barrage of media messages and images in the last decade informing the public that behavior is biologically dictated. There is a daily drumbeat emanating from the TV and the newspapers informing us that behavior is genetic, hardwired, strictly biological. Newspapers, which hardly reported health news thirty years ago, report study after study showing that behavior is biologically inherited and determined. Headlines scream "Man's Genes Made Him Kill, His Lawyers Claim," or ask "Are Your Genes to Blame?" . . .

Popular Psychiatry

This incessant *physicalizing* of behavior—which allows for a broken mind to be seen in roughly the same terms as a broken leg—has softened the image of psychological disturbance in general, and mental illness in particular. In this context, madness has, at times, become alluring and inviting and, at the very least, enormously popular. [American author] Sylvia Plath was remarkably prescient when she noted in her journal, while contemplating writing *The Bell Jar,* that "there's an increasing market for mental-hospital stuff."

To be sure, the most common portrayal of mental illness, both in the movies and in the headlines, is still the violent schizophrenic. But given its sordid history, the image of mental illness has quite improbably and suddenly become nearly chic. We have seen an emergence of "psychiatric chic," akin to the "heroin chic" of models and downtown artists. . . .

Shifting Statistics

In 1996, 38 percent of Americans viewed depression as a health problem, as opposed to a sign of personal weakness. By 2006, 72 percent saw depression as a health problem. In general, Americans feel much closer to mental dysfunction. In 1957, one in five Americans reported having personal fears of an impending nervous breakdown; by 1996, it was one in four.

Americans adore their prescription drugs like no other people on earth, but they really, really adore their psychiatric drugs.

In this environment, then, it is not at all surprising that Americans think that they are much crazier than people in other countries. In 2004, the World Health Organization completed a study on the global prevalence of mental illness. Based on structured, in-home interviews, an extraordinary *26 percent* of Americans reported that they suffered from any type of psychiatric disorder in the prior year—far exceeding the rates of all of the other fifteen countries. By contrast, 5 percent of Nigerians, 8 percent of Italians, 9 percent of Germans, and 12 percent of Mexicans reported having a psychiatric disorder. (The only country that came close to the United States was perennially troubled Ukraine.) Americans described themselves as being particularly vulnerable to anxiety disorders and impulse-control disorders, reporting them at double the rates of every other country but Colombia and France. Almost 8 percent of Americans reported having suffered from a serious mental disorder, a rate about three times higher than any other developed country in the survey. In reporting the story, the *New York Times* stated, bluntly, about Americans: "Most Will Be Mentally Ill at Some Point, Study Says." "We lead the world in a lot of good things, but we're also leaders in this one particular domain that we'd rather not be," said the study's lead author.

Deeply Immersed in Craziness

Americans have responded to what's in the air, and on the air, around them. They are deeply immersed in craziness. They take drugs for their perceived insanity at rates far exceeding any other country; they make movies and watch TV shows about mental illness like never before; they talk about mental illness in a newfound language; and they think they are the craziest people on earth.

Americans have the most luridly expensive urine in the world.

And indeed all this drug taking is a profoundly, even outrageously, American phenomenon. Americans adore their prescription drugs like no other people on earth, but they really, really adore their psychiatric drugs. Americans are responsible for almost half of the world's prescription drug sales, but the disparity is even greater when it comes to CNS (central nervous system) agents. In 2006, Americans—about 6 percent of the world's population—bought about two-thirds of the world's psychiatric and neurological drugs. In 2006, 66 percent of the global antidepressant market was accounted for by the United States. And in 2003 approximately 83 percent of the global market for attention deficit hyperactivity disorder medications was accounted for by the United States, and mainly by U.S. children. . . .

This is not to say that mental illness isn't, in essence, a product of problematic neurotransmitters and faulty brain functioning—the evidence is overwhelming that it is—and that these drugs aren't extraordinarily effective at times for the people they were developed for, people with severe psychiatric conditions. It is and they are. I have witnessed the lifesaving impact of the drugs for people who really need them, people with true medical illnesses like schizophrenia, bipolar disorder, and major depression. Many of the severely ill clients that I worked with would not have survived without the drugs. But in our characteristic American impatience and zeal, the drugs have been hyped beyond the limits of their ability to help most people; their efficacy with very specific populations has been overgeneralized and misapplied to treat the troubles of the masses generally and upper-middle-class angst specifically; their largely unknown mechanisms of action have been made, literally, into cartoons; and their subtleties have been ignored and side effects overlooked.

Americans have swallowed it all—literally. To say that we are the most medicated nation on earth is an absurd understatement. To say that we are the most psychiatrically medicated nation on earth is a prodigiously absurd understatement. Americans have the most luridly expensive urine in the world.

4

ADHD Drugs Are Overprescribed for Children

Linda Marsa

Linda Marsa is a Los Angeles–based investigative journalist, author, and teacher specializing in science, medicine, and health.

Some 4 million American children are currently diagnosed as having attention-deficit/hyperactivity disorder (ADHD), and they consume 31 million drug prescriptions annually to combat symptoms such as disruptive or impulsive behavior, restlessness, and lack of focus. When kids act out in school, teachers, counselors, and family physicians are often quick to recommend medication to make them easier to manage. The United States uses 80 percent of the world's Ritalin, a stimulant drug for ADHD, a statistic many attribute to an overly permissive society that medicates children rather than disciplining them. While some children are truly helped by ADHD drugs, many children may not need such medication at all. The symptoms of ADHD can also come from other disorders, such as learning and information-processing deficiencies, or even stressful family situations like abuse or divorce. Giving children powerful ADHD medications rather than fully exploring behavioral problems and trying other interventions first is bad medicine, and parents should be wary of starting their kids on such drugs.

It's a rare parent today who's not familiar with the term attention deficit/hyperactivity disorder, or ADHD. Indeed, this once-obscure abbreviation is now a household word, thanks in part to the fact that the number of kids diagnosed with the condition has skyrocketed—from an estimated 150,000 in 1970, to a half million in 1985, to a whopping four million currently [as of 2005]. (It is outranked only by asthma and allergies among childhood disorders.)

Predictably, prescriptions for ADHD treatments have ballooned proportionately, rising more than 47 percent over the past five years to a current total of 31 million. The ADHD therapeutic arsenal—a $2.2-billion-a-year business—now includes a dozen drugs, the use of which has steadily drifted downward to ever-younger children.

A landmark 2000 *Journal of the American Medical Association* study revealed that use among 2- to 4-year-olds of stimulants such as Ritalin (which, paradoxically, have a calming effect on hyperactive kids) nearly tripled from 1991 to 1995; Ritalin prescriptions for preschoolers rose 49 percent from 2000 to 2003. This is especially sobering in view of the fact that Ritalin is not even approved for use in children under 6; all these prescriptions are written off-label [i.e., for other than originally approved uses].

We medicate our kids more, and for more trivial reasons, than any other culture. We'd rather give them a pill than discipline them.

Is Medication Really Necessary?

Despite the galloping increase in the use of such drugs, there is still considerable confusion as to exactly what ADHD is and how it should be treated. Part of the problem is that there is no definitive test to certify that a child has it. And because symptoms run the gamut from constant frenzied activity and disruptive, impulsive behavior to fidgeting, making careless mistakes in schoolwork, and failing to finish tasks, it's not always easy to distinguish between normal kid behavior and

ADHD. Diagnosis is still a judgment call, says Timothy E. Wilens, MD, author of *Straight Talk About Psychiatric Medications for Kids*.

In addition, the spectrum of ADHD has broadened. There are now thought to be three distinct types. The most extreme—and the one most associated with the label—is the hyperactive, impulsive child who is disruptive, can't sit still, and may be a bully or a troublemaker. Children with the second type are those who are inattentive, unable to focus, and easily distracted. The third type, and the most common one, usually combines inattention and hyperactivity.

For children whose extreme impulsivity and aggressiveness cause them to fall hopelessly behind in school and to become social outcasts, a parent's decision to medicate can be painful but clear-cut. But what about the parents of the millions of other kids who also bear the ADHD label but whose behavior is more ambiguous? These parents face thorny questions: Is their child's energy, dreaminess, or inattentiveness merely normal youthful behavior, or does it cross the line into a neurological illness? And would putting the child on drugs be a help or the chemical equivalent of handcuffs?

Behavioral pediatrician Lawrence H. Diller, MD, author of *Running on Ritalin*, believes the latter. "America uses 80 percent of the world's Ritalin," he says. "We medicate our kids more, and for more trivial reasons, than any other culture. We'd rather give them a pill than discipline them." His view is shared by many others, who chalk up the seemingly limitless numbers of antsy, disruptive kids to the failures of a permissive society that can't control its children and babysits them with MTV.

Others pointedly disagree. "ADHD has not increased, we're just identifying it better," says Steven Pliszka, MD, chief of child psychiatry at the University of Texas Health Science Center, in San Antonio. "In the past, these kids were the ones who were always being sent to the principal's office." Moreover, research shows that there is a strong genetic component to the disorder. If a child has it, the odds are good that a parent may, too (though he or she may be unaware of it).

It is easier and cheaper for a doctor to simply prescribe a pill than to direct the child to costly therapists.

But even if the data strongly suggest a biological origin to ADHD, says William E. Pelham Jr., PhD, director of the Center for Children and Families at the State University of New York at Buffalo, there is little doubt that environmental factors can nudge a latent, largely benign tendency into a full-blown disorder requiring medication. Several trends in American life have converged to whip up this perfect storm.

Schools Are Ground Zero for ADHD

Let's start with our schools. Faced with steadily dwindling resources and the need to find time for everything in state-mandated curricula, many have curtailed gym classes, even recess, where energetic kids can let off steam. Teachers, already pushed to the limit, are often unable to handle a "trouble-maker" who creates chaos in their crowded classrooms—in turn putting parents under pressure to make their child conform. (Three-quarters of initial referrals for an ADHD examination originate with teachers, not parents.)

"Teachers are good at spotting a child who's different," says Mina K. Dulcan, MD, head of child and adolescent psychiatry at Northwestern University's Feinberg School of Medicine, in Chicago. And in doing so, they perform a valuable service. But it's valid to wonder whether, in the words of Barbara M. Korsch, MD, a professor of pediatrics at the University of Southern California, in Los Angeles, "we're giving youngsters Ritalin as a solution for poor classroom behavior."

Our healthcare system also helps make medication a likelier solution. Because HMOs [health maintenance organizations] and managed-care plans often either explicitly or implicitly encourage primary-care physicians to limit referrals to specialists, it is easier and cheaper for a doctor simply to prescribe a pill than to direct the child to costly therapists.

Others point the finger at the beleaguered institution of the modern family itself, with its (commonly) two working parents who may lack the stamina to create a highly structured home environment and who may not restrict television, video games, or Internet access. Indeed, a 2004 University of Washington study indicated a link between early exposure to television and attention problems in children.

Add to this mix the fact that, in the early 1990s, kids with ADHD who meet certain criteria became eligible for special services from their schools, which has meant that more kids were identified. And the debut of a new drug is usually accompanied by intensive sales campaigns aimed at doctors and TV viewers. "New drugs always mean more people get medication," explains Dr. Pelham.

ADHD Is Hard to Diagnose

Even when a child's symptoms clearly point to something beyond the normal vicissitudes of childhood, ADHD can be tricky to pin down. Depression, anxiety, bipolar disorder, dyslexia, learning disabilities, even impaired hearing or vision, can be mistaken for ADHD because the symptoms (insomnia, impulsiveness, inattention) are similar.

Other factors that can spark ADHD-like behaviors include emotional disruptions (divorce, the death of a close relative, a parent's job loss), neglect or abuse, an unstructured home environment, and medical problems such as epilepsy or hyperthyroidism. Sleep apnea also triggers ADHD-like symptoms, according to recent research by Ronald Chervin, MD, a sleep researcher at the University of Michigan, in Ann Arbor. "If kids don't get undisturbed sleep," he says, "they're naturally going to be inattentive and less able to learn."

The obvious first step in helping a child is to obtain an accurate diagnosis. Given the murkiness of ADHD, such accuracy requires several hours of careful evaluation, not a 15-minute office visit and a rush to medicate because a teacher complains that a child is disruptive. As tempting as it may be to give a child a pill to see whether he improves, this is poor medical practice. As Dr. Wilens notes, a positive response to a Ritalin-like stimulant does not mean a child has ADHD— these drugs can have the effect of making anyone who takes them more focused (ask any college student who has used Ritalin to cram for finals). . . .

American Academy of Pediatrics Guidelines

To help experts distinguish ADHD from other conditions, the American Academy of Pediatrics have devised guidelines, including the following:

- Symptoms must meet the criteria for the disorder established by the American Psychiatric Association. . . .

- Behaviors must create a genuine impairment in at least two areas of the child's life. If the only problem is in the classroom, it is more likely to be a learning disability than ADHD.

- Symptoms must have persisted for at least six months and have seriously interfered with the child's friendships, school activities, home life, and overall functioning.

Such evaluations typically cost anywhere from $600 to $2,000 and may be covered by health insurance. Federal law also requires [a] public school to provide both free evaluations and remedial classes for eligible kids with ADHD. . . .

A Story of Misdiagnosis

Patricia Mark's son Nicholas was diagnosed with ADHD at age 8, after his third-grade teacher noticed he didn't pay attention, had trouble reading, and wrote illegibly. "He'd have these momentary staring spells," recalls Mark, 45, a mother of three in New Milford, Connecticut. "And though he could spell any word in his head, the letters would be all jumbled when he put them on paper."

The school district referred her to a psychologist, who attributed Nicholas's symptoms to ADHD and suggested he take Ritalin. Convinced in her gut that this diagnosis was wrong, Mark refused to give her son drugs. She spent six years consulting one specialist after another. Finally, a neurologist ordered a brain scan, which revealed that Nicholas suffered from mild epilepsy. Earlier tests indicated he also had dyslexia.

Tutoring and special-education classes have helped Nicholas cope with his learning disability, but Mark feels that the boy, now a senior in high school, will never recover academically from the years he lost. Still, she remains grateful that she trusted her instincts. "Ritalin can trigger seizures," she says. "If I had done what the 'experts' advised, it might have killed him."

Drugs Can Turn a Child's Life Around

From the moment her daughter, Juliet, was born, Leslie Pia knew she was different from other babies. She cried inconsolably, rarely slept, refused to stay in her stroller, and buzzed with nervous energy. By age 2, Juliet's fierce temper tantrums made her a social pariah among her peers. "None of the mothers wanted her around their children," recalls Pia, an event planner in Plainview, New York. As the terrible twos progressed into the even-worse threes, Pia realized that Juliet wasn't going to outgrow her erratic behavior, so she and her husband, Steven, had her evaluated by a private psychologist. The verdict: Juliet suffered from ADHD.

The psychologists broached the possibility of medication, but the Pias were adamantly opposed. "I was appalled at the idea of a child barely out of diapers popping these powerful pills," says Pia, who notes that even experts are unsure what long-term effects these medications may have, especially when they're given at such a key stage of neurological development (the brain undergoes the majority of its growth during the first five years of life).

Instead, Pia scaled back her work schedule to spend more time with her daughter, read everything she could find about ADHD, and learned behavior-modification techniques. She even tried occupational therapy to tame her unruly child, who wandered around during circle time at her nursery school, bullied her classmates on the playground, and had trouble transitioning calmly from one activity to another.

"These methods would work temporarily, but nothing had a lasting effect—her brain and body were just moving too fast," Pia says. "Since I couldn't sit in the classroom with her all day long, nursery school was just a horror."

As Juliet prepared to enter kindergarten, the desperate couple made the "harrowing decision" to give their daughter the stimulant Concerta. As heart-wrenching as it was to "give my 5-year-old a pill in her applesauce," recalls Pia, the effects were immediate and dramatic. Suddenly, Juliet could sit calmly and do her work without making a fuss; she could play peacefully for short periods with other kids.

The girl, now 7, still attends behavioral therapy to improve her social skills, but "there is just no comparison to the way she was before," marvels her mom.

Parents Face Pressure to Medicate Kids

Sheila Matthews's nightmare began when her son entered first grade. His teacher phoned regularly to complain about the boy's disruptive behavior—he would blurt out answers and refuse to sit still. His teacher assigned him a special seat away from his classmates and used negative and positive reinforcements to try to curb his disruptions.

"All she was doing was stigmatizing and humiliating him," recalls Matthews, a mother of two in New Canaan, Connecticut. "This was a kid who had loved school and was always excited about learning. Suddenly he was telling me he hated school and hated himself. He was only 6!"

In all but the most severe cases, ADHD can be treated as effectively with intensive behavioral coaching as with medicine.

The school psychologist diagnosed the boy with ADHD and urged his parents to consider medication. "The psychologist told me, 'if you don't medicate him, research shows he'll self-medicate with drugs and alcohol,'" says Matthews. "I was frightened and horrified." Convinced the school district was trying to sedate her son to make him easier to manage, Matthews stood firm.

She believed her child was merely outgoing and energetic, and that drugs would dampen his natural high spirits. Instead, she paid $2,000 for an evaluation by a private psychologist, who determined the boy had trouble with sequencing, reasoning, and comprehension. This diagnosis qualified him for special speech and language services through the school district. She also enrolled him in an after-school program in third and fourth grades that helped build communication skills.

Her persistence paid off. Her son, now 12, is bringing home B's on his seventh-grade report card and learning to play guitar. "When he started doing better academically, his behavioral problems diminished," Matthews says.

In all but the most severe cases, ADHD can be treated as effectively with intensive behavioral coaching as with medicine, according to advocates such as Dr. Pelham. Most no-drug programs emphasize the use of goal setting, organizational skills, and time management. Children with ADHD need consistent rules, a high degree of daily structure, and stern consequences for misbehavior. . . .

Side Effects of ADHD Drugs

ADHD medications work by changing the levels of brain chemicals such as dopamine and norepinephrine, which help modulate activity in the parts of the brain that regulate attention, impulse control, motor activity, and organization. But what do these drugs do to [a] child's body?

While medication is sometimes the only answer for kids with severe ADHD, it's important to realize that these drugs can carry serious side effects, including insomnia, appetite loss, upset stomachs, and tics—and even, according to the most recent research, possible depression in adults who took Ritalin as kids. A small percentage of kids are also vulnerable to a "rebound effect" when the drugs wear off in the late afternoon and symptoms resurface.

While medication is sometimes the only answer for kids with severe ADHD, it's important to realize that these drugs can carry serious side effects.

Experts point out, however, that this problem has largely been eliminated in recent years. In rare instances, youngsters may experience seizures, or their growth may be affected when they continuously take medication. Most experts advise against the continuous use of these medications, especially for years on end. And many advocate that [a] child take a medically supervised "vacation" from medication at least once a year to see how he or she fares without it.

5

ADHD Drugs Are Appropriately Prescribed for Children

Hannah Seligson

Hannah Seligson is an author and journalist based in New York City.

Investigative journalist Judith Warner set out to write a book about the overdiagnosis and overmedication of American children for attention-deficit disorder (ADD) or attention-deficit/ hyperactivity disorder (ADHD) and other mental health issues, but when she started doing research for the book, she concluded that kids are not overmedicated at all. According to the National Institute of Mental Health, only about 5 percent of American children take some type of psychiatric medication, and just 3 to 5 percent have an ADHD diagnosis. The media are responsible for raising a false alarm and perpetuating the myth that children are being improperly medicated. One reason the number of children on medications is growing is because of better diagnostic testing and treatment options. While many other therapies are available for ADHD and other disorders, they cannot entirely replace medication for most children. Parents who choose medication for their children understand that the benefits outweigh the risks.

A ren't all kids on some kind of medication? Isn't everyone diagnosed with something these days? Isn't ADD as common as the sniffles?

Not really, says Judith Warner, author of the new book *We've Got Issues: Children and Parents in the Age of Medication*. Warner is best known for outing the culture of over-parenting in her first book, *Perfect Madness: Motherhood in the Age of Anxiety*, and her Domestic Disturbances column on *The New York Times* Web site, and now she's decided to quiet the cacophony of misconceptions about children, medication, overdiagnosing, and overmedicating in one confident hush.

How does Warner do it? She starts by challenging her own beliefs.

When she began writing her book, almost five years ago [in 2005], she came to it thinking the narratives the media had spun about children and medication were true: Parents were trying to "perfect" their children through various cocktails of medications; doctors were going prescription-happy; and kids who occasionally got sad were being labeled "depressed."

Assumptions Not Borne Out

"Those assumptions, however, weren't borne out by clinicians, parents, children, or statistics," says Warner, who did lots of research to support her thesis.

Here's what the numbers teach us:

About 5 percent of kids take psychiatric medication and, depending on how one reads the data, anywhere between 5 and 20 percent of kids today have mental-health issues. We are not a Ritalin nation. According to The National Institute of Mental Health, attention deficit disorder occurs in about 3 to 5 percent of school-age children.

The overmedicated and overdiagnosed child, Warner argues, is a media embellishment. And it's become an obsession and storyline that eclipses the realities.

We've Got Issues spotlights a bigger problem: the lack of medical care for many children with mental issues. With an overwhelmed mental-health industry—there are only 7,000 child psychiatrists in the U.S., mostly concentrated in urban areas—those who need help often don't get it. Mental-health issues have been portrayed as a bourgeois malady because that is the only segment of our population that can afford to have them. The full battery of tests to get a diagnosis costs about $2,000, which insurance companies often do not reimburse. Warner takes a stab at offering some policy solutions, including a clarion call for insurance companies to reimburse families for diagnostic tests and to increase the number of child psychiatrists.

She quotes John March, a Duke University psychiatrist, as saying, "Child psychiatry will really be the heart of psychiatry in the future. Epidemiology now shows that if you're mentally ill as an adult, you first were mentally ill as a child or an adolescent."

We've Got Issues is a reality check that separates the perceived outrages from the genuine ones, and for this alone Warner provides a real service.

The increased diagnosis and treatment for ADHD may be a major public health success story.

Areas of Controversy Still Remain

Warner is saying "bring it on" to all the dicey, controversial, and murky areas that obscure the subject of children and medication, and she's not afraid to acknowledge the issues on which there isn't consensus, including whether there really are more children with mental issues today than there were 30 years ago. "I don't know if there really are more, or we are just recognizing them more," says Warner.

Still, she devotes a chapter to exploring the topic. One of the more intriguing explanations is "assortative mating," a theory that researchers say could be one explanation for the mysterious surge of autism in our time. The theory is that today kids are getting a "higher genetic load" because people are now marrying mates who are similar to them. "Even one generation back you didn't have a physicist marrying a physicist," says Warner. Dr. Demitri Papolos, an associate professor of psychiatry at the Albert Einstein College of Medicine, says that in the past "spousal selection took into consideration knowledge of the partner's family . . . now few couples have much of a clue as to the medical and psychiatric history of families they are marrying into."

A Thoughtful Look at Medication

As for medication, Warner doesn't get righteous; she looks at the facts.

In 2005, Darshak Sanghavi, chief of pediatric cardiology and an assistant professor of pediatrics at the University of Massachusetts Medical School, wrote a piece for *The Boston Globe* under the headline "Time to calm down about Ritalin," arguing "the increased diagnosis and treatment of ADHD may be a major public health success story."

A lot of medications do work, not all parents are making their children into sacrificial lambs to their own ambitions, and a number of children do suffer from mental health issues.

Taking Warner's trademark nuanced tone, *We've Got Issues* comes down on Sanghavi's side. "I talked to one doctor who is trying to retrain the cerebellum, I talked to one doctor who believes in transcendental meditation, and I have read about many other alternative treatments, and all of them said these therapies can supplement medication, but most of the time for most children they don't end up replacing medication entirely," says Warner.

Statistics and studies aside, Warner humanizes the issues for the reader. Throughout the book she introduces parents of children whose lives were saved by medication: children who used to scream and kick for four hours while they did their homework were able, with the help of the right medication, to do it in half the time without the temper tantrums; children who might never have been able to emancipate (read: go to college) if they hadn't been on mood stabilizers.

Validating Parents' Experiences

Warner, however, is anything but glib—that's virtually impossible in a book that has close to 50 pages of notes—about medication, and *We've Got Issues* certainly isn't a paean to the prescription pad, but, like a good journalist, she sees it from all sides.

"I can understand why parents think medication is scary," she says. "It hasn't been around long enough and it can have terrible side effects, but many parents get to a point where they feel it is unfair to the child not to be on the medication, where they come to feel the benefits outweigh the risks."

The book is most successful at changing the narrative about children with mental-health issues. Of course there are pill-pushing parents, overdiagnosing psychologists, fraudulent drug companies, and irresponsible doctors, but there's another truth that Warner shakes out: A lot of medications do work, not all parents are making their children into sacrificial lambs to their own ambitions, and a number of children do suffer from mental health issues. Parents will find solace in seeing their own experiences validated on Warner's pages.

6

Ads Do Not Significantly Increase Demand for Unneeded Medications

Brian Alexander

Brian Alexander is a California-based writer who covers health issues for msnbc.com. He is the author of Rapture: How Biotech Became the New Religion.

Pharmaceutical companies spend more than $5 billion annually to advertise prescription drugs in the United States. The practice has been heavily criticized by those who believe the ads entice people to ask their doctors for unnecessary or ineffective drugs—and that doctors, in turn, are likely to prescribe them. But a recent study shows that the public is less influenced by drug advertising than it used to be. The study found that—despite the ever-increasing number of drug ads—half as many patients requested prescriptions for specific drugs when they visited their doctors in 2009 than they did in 2003.

The pharmaceutical industry says this shows that the primary effect of prescription drug advertising is not selling more drugs, but patient education that positively increases people's awareness of diseases, symptoms, and possible treatments.

Watching TV news could make you think America faces a crisis of irritable bowels, malfunctioning genitals and insomnia. The pharmaceutical industry spends billions of dollars each year to make sure you know about these, and other, conditions.

But a new study appears to show that all those direct-to-consumer ads for prescription drugs to treat such conditions have much less effect than previously thought, a finding that could be bad news for pharmaceutical companies and the media outlets with which they advertise.

Only 3.5 percent of patient visits to a group of Colorado doctors' offices and public health clinics included a patient request for a prescription for a specific drug, says the study, published in the *Annals of Family Medicine*. This was about half the rate reported in a somewhat comparable study from 2003.

The marketing of prescription medications has been controversial since 1997, when the government loosened restrictions on drug ads. Prescription drug advertising, allowed only in the United States and New Zealand, has exploded in the years since. It now tops $5 billion annually, according to a report by TNS Media Intelligence, a marketing research firm, though spending began falling off in 2007.

Advertising Sparks Debate

Debate about the practice has exploded, too. Drug companies argue that advertising medications provides an important public health service by alerting consumers to potentially undiagnosed, or undertreated, disorders. Some doctors and health advocates, on the other hand, argue that ads entice patients to insist on unnecessary or ineffective drugs and to forgo healthy lifestyle changes that might obviate the need for drugs in the first place.

The new study supports both sides.

Twenty-two primary care practices in Colorado participated. The researchers surveyed 1,647 "patient encounters"—appointments. During those appointments, 58 patients, or 3.5 percent, asked about obtaining a prescription for a specific drug. When the data was sifted to include only queries about specific drugs that had been advertised in recent years, the number fell to 43, or 2.6 percent.

Not Doctor's First Choice

Importantly, when a patient did ask about a specific drug, that drug was usually not the doctor's first choice of treatment. "Nevertheless," the study found, "the physician prescribed the [requested] medication about one-half the time."

This does not necessarily mean doctors are caving in and practicing bad medicine, said Dr. Richard Kravitz, a professor and vice-chair of research in the Department of Internal Medicine at the University of California–Davis, and an investigator on the 2003 study.

"It might be bad if it is more costly, but it is not as bad clinically as it sounds," Kravitz explained. "A lot of decisions in medicine have no clear right or wrong."

Indeed, doctors in the new study described the "overall effect of the patient request as neutral or positive in 90 percent of the visits."

The study's lead author, Dr. Bennett Parnes, an associate professor of family medicine at the University of Colorado School of Medicine, described the results as surprising. "It is not the dreaded event where you have to deal with a patient who wants medications the provider does not want to prescribe. It is just not happening that much."

Patient Education Is the Result

Half the time there was a specific patient drug request, Parnes said, a new condition was identified and there was "some patient education going on. That's not a bad thing."

But Dr. Lisa Schwartz, an associate professor of medicine at Dartmouth Medical School who has long studied consumer drug advertising, isn't persuaded. She pointed out that the Parnes study population, which included a number of community health centers serving a low-income population, may not be the best measure. Such health centers often have limited drug choices, and the patients may not have had as much exposure to drug ads.

"(That) makes it hard to make strong inferences that direct-to-consumer advertising does not work," Schwartz said.

Worrying about frequency of requests may miss the point, she said. It may be more important to know if consumers who do request a drug truly understand what they're asking for. Many ads, she argued, do not include enough information on how well drugs work.

"If it is supposed to be educational for consumers, why doesn't the ad contain that piece of information?" she said.

In the wake of recalls for drugs like Vioxx, Americans may be more skeptical of what they see advertised.

The sleep drug Lunesta, for example, advertised with a gentle moth floating in through a bedroom window, gets patients to sleep 15 minutes faster after six months of treatment and provides 37 minutes more sleep per night. Patients ought to have that information, she said, to help judge whether the cost is justified.

Consumers Are More Discerning

Parnes speculated that if the rate of requests for drugs is falling, it could be because Americans and their doctors have become inured to drug advertising. "Clinicians 10 years ago may have been shocked by a patient asking, but now they are comfortable with hearing it and responding to it and patients overall are more empowered than 10 years ago."

Plus, in the wake of recalls for drugs like Vioxx, Americans may be more skeptical of what they see advertised, he said.

Kravitz, who has done studies showing higher request rates than Parnes' work demonstrates, remains suspicious of a general drop. He agreed with Parnes that the nature of the ads themselves has changed. There are more ads for extremely expensive drugs like Humira, a medication for rheumatoid arthritis, and for less common conditions, he said. Both could limit requests.

Ads Are Conversation Starters

The new research is not likely to quell calls to ban drug ads. In 2007, Dr. Kurt Stange, the editor of the *Annals of Family Medicine*, declared it "time to ban direct-to-consumer advertising of prescription drugs" because such ads "provide biased educational material and emotional appeals that promote drugs over healthy alternatives."

Of course, those are claims the industry vigorously disputes.

Regulated by the federal Food and Drug Administration, direct-to-consumer advertising "increases people's awareness of disease and available treatments," according to online guidelines from the Pharmaceutical Research and Manufacturers of America [PhRMA], a drugmakers' trade group. Because of the advertising, patients may be more likely to talk to their doctors, PhRMA contends.

"It fosters an informed conversation about health, disease and treatments between patients and their health care practitioners," the guidelines suggest.

7

Low-Income Children Are More Likely to Be Prescribed Psychiatric Drugs

Duff Wilson

Duff Wilson is a staff writer for the New York Times.

Low-income American children who receive health care through the government's Medicaid program are four times more likely to be given powerful antipsychotic medications for mental and behavioral problems than more affluent children who have private health insurance. In addition, they are more likely to be given the drugs for less severe conditions and to be given drugs to treat conditions for which the drugs are not approved. Part of the reason for this disparity is that Medicaid typically pays in full for such drugs but not for counseling or psychotherapy, which can be just as effective, and low-income families are less likely to be able to afford to pursue those options on their own. Some experts think that the stresses of poverty, single-parent homes, poorer schools, and lack of access to preventive health care that many low-income families face may also play a role in shaping the statistics.

New federally financed drug research reveals a stark disparity: children covered by Medicaid are given powerful antipsychotic medicines at a rate four times higher than children whose parents have private insurance. And the Medicaid children are more likely to receive the drugs for less severe conditions than their middle-class counterparts, the data shows.

Those findings, by a team from Rutgers and Columbia, are almost certain to add fuel to a long-running debate. Do too many children from poor families receive powerful psychiatric drugs not because they actually need them—but because it is deemed the most efficient and cost-effective way to control problems that may be handled much differently for middle-class children?

The questions go beyond the psychological impact on Medicaid children, serious as that may be. Antipsychotic drugs can also have severe physical side effects, causing drastic weight gain and metabolic changes resulting in lifelong physical problems.

Children with diagnoses of mental or emotional problems in low-income families are more likely to be given drugs than receive family counseling or psychotherapy.

On Tuesday [December 8, 2009], a pediatric advisory committee to the Food and Drug Administration [F.D.A.] met to discuss the health risks for all children who take antipsychotics. The panel will consider recommending new label warnings for the drugs, which are now used by hundreds of thousands of people under age 18 in this country, counting both Medicaid patients and those with private insurance.

Meanwhile, a group of Medicaid medical directors from 16 states, under a project they call Too Many, Too Much, Too Young, has been experimenting with ways to reduce prescriptions of antipsychotic drugs among Medicaid children.

They plan to publish a report early next year [2010].

The Rutgers-Columbia study will also be published early [in 2010], in the peer-reviewed journal *Health Affairs*. But the findings have already been posted on the Web, setting off discussion among experts who treat and study troubled young people.

Experts Stunned by Disparity

Some experts say they are stunned by the disparity in prescribing patterns. But others say it reinforces previous indications, and their own experience, that children with diagnoses of mental or emotional problems in low-income families are more likely to be given drugs than receive family counseling or psychotherapy.

Part of the reason is insurance reimbursements, as Medicaid often pays much less for counseling and therapy than private insurers do. Part of it may have to do with the challenges that families in poverty may have in consistently attending counseling or therapy sessions, even when such help is available.

"It's easier for patients, and it's easier for docs," said Dr. Derek H. Suite, a psychiatrist in the Bronx whose pediatric cases include children and adolescents covered by Medicaid and who sometimes prescribes antipsychotics. "But the question is, 'What are you prescribing it for?' That's where it gets a little fuzzy."

Too often, Dr. Suite said, he sees young Medicaid patients to whom other doctors have given antipsychotics that the patients do not seem to need. Recently, for example, he met with a 15-year-old girl. She had stopped taking the antipsychotic medication that had been prescribed for her after a single examination, paid for by Medicaid, at a clinic where she received a diagnosis of bipolar disorder.

Why did she stop? Dr. Suite asked. "I can control my moods," the girl said softly.

After evaluating her, Dr. Suite decided she was right. The girl had arguments with her mother and stepfather and some insomnia. But she was a good student and certainly not bipolar, in Dr. Suite's opinion.

"Normal teenager," Dr. Suite said, nodding. "No scrips [prescriptions] for you."

Because there can be long waits to see the psychiatrists accepting Medicaid, it is often a pediatrician or family doctor who prescribes an antipsychotic to a Medicaid patient— whether because the parent wants it or the doctor believes there are few other options.

Though [antipsychotic] drugs are typically cheaper than long-term therapy, they are the single biggest drug expenditure for Medicaid.

Some experts even say Medicaid may provide better care for children than many covered by private insurance because the drugs—which can cost $400 a month—are provided free to patients, and families do not have to worry about the copayments and other insurance restrictions.

"Maybe Medicaid kids are getting better treatment," said Dr. Gabrielle Carlson, a child psychiatrist and professor at the [State University of New York at] Stony Brook School of Medicine. "If it helps keep them in school, maybe it's not so bad."

Medicaid Drug Costs Could Grow

In any case, as Congress works on health care legislation that could expand the nation's Medicaid rolls by 15 million people—a 43 percent increase—the scope of the antipsychotics problem, and the expense, could grow in coming years.

Even though the drugs are typically cheaper than long-term therapy, they are the single biggest drug expenditure for Medicaid, costing the program $7.9 billion in 2006, the most recent year for which the data is available.

The Rutgers-Columbia research, based on millions of Medicaid and private insurance claims, is the most extensive analysis of its type yet on children's antipsychotic drug use. It examined records for children in seven big states—including

New York, Texas and California—selected to be representative of the nation's Medicaid population, for the years 2001 and 2004.

The data indicated that more than 4 percent of patients aged 6 to 17 in Medicaid fee-for-service programs received antipsychotic drugs, compared with less than 1 percent of privately insured children and adolescents. More recent data through 2007 indicates that the disparity has remained, said Stephen Crystal, a Rutgers professor who led the study.

Other Factors May Contribute

Experts generally agree that some characteristics of the Medicaid population may contribute to psychological problems or psychiatric disorders. They include the stresses of poverty, single-parent homes, poorer schools, lack of access to preventive care and the fact that the Medicaid rolls include many adults who are themselves mentally ill.

As a result, studies have found that children in low-income families may have a higher rate of mental health problems— perhaps two to one—compared with children in better-off families. But that still does not explain the four-to-one disparity in prescribing antipsychotics.

Professor Crystal, who is the director of the Center for Pharmacotherapy at Rutgers, says his team's data also indicates that poorer children are more likely to receive antipsychotics for less serious conditions than would typically prompt a prescription for a middle-class child.

But Professor Crystal said he did not have clear evidence to form an opinion on whether or not children on Medicaid were being overtreated.

"Medicaid kids are subject to a lot of stresses that lead to behavior issues which can be hard to distinguish from more serious psychiatric conditions," he said. "It's very hard to pin down."

And yet Dr. Mark Olfson, a psychiatry professor at Columbia and a co-author of the study, said at least one thing was clear: "A lot of these kids are not getting other mental health services."

Medicaid children were more likely than those with private insurance to be given the drugs for off-label uses like A.D.H.D.

Off-Label Uses Common

The F.D.A. has approved antipsychotic drugs for children specifically to treat schizophrenia, autism and bipolar disorder. But they are more frequently prescribed to children for other, less extreme conditions, including attention deficit hyperactivity disorder [A.D.H.D.], aggression, persistent defiance or other so-called conduct disorders—especially when the children are covered by Medicaid, the new study shows.

Although doctors may legally prescribe the drugs for these "off label" uses, there have been no long-term studies of their effects when used for such conditions.

The Rutgers-Columbia study found that Medicaid children were more likely than those with private insurance to be given the drugs for off-label uses like A.D.H.D. and conduct disorders. The privately insured children, in turn, were more likely than their Medicaid counterparts to receive the drugs for F.D.A.-approved uses like bipolar disorder.

Even if parents enrolled in Medicaid may be reluctant to put their children on drugs, some come to rely on them as the only thing that helps.

"They say it's impossible to stop now," Evelyn Torres, 48, of the Bronx, said of her son's use of antipsychotics since he received a diagnosis of bipolar disorder at age 3. Seven years later, the boy is now also afflicted with weight and heart problems. But Ms. Torres credits Medicaid for making the boy's mental and physical conditions manageable. "They're helping with everything," she said.

8

Wichita Witch Hunt— The Justice Department Wages War on Pain Relief

Harvey Silverglate

Harvey Silverglate, author of Three Felonies a Day: How the Feds Target the Innocent, *is a criminal defense and civil liberties attorney in Cambridge, Massachusetts.*

People who have painful chronic conditions have a hard time finding doctors who will prescribe enough medication to help them adequately manage their pain because federal narcotics officers are increasingly arresting and prosecuting doctors—especially those who specialize in pain management—for prescribing too many heavy narcotics to patients. The Drug Enforcement Administration does not seem to understand that patients can develop tolerance to their pain drugs over time so a higher dose may be needed to achieve the same results. Since 2003 more than four hundred doctors have been criminally prosecuted for their pain management prescriptions. In addition, the government has also tried to silence patient advocates who publicly argue for effective pain management. Because physicians are frightened of legal action, Americans who have chronic pain often do not receive enough medication to alleviate their suffering.

No good deed goes unpunished when a private citizen is up against the federal drug warriors—those members of the Department of Justice who have been seeking, with in-

Harvey Silverglate, "Wichita Witch Hunt—The Justice Department Wages War on Pain Relief," Forbes.com, September 1, 2009. Reprinted by Permission of Forbes Media LLC © 2010.

creasing success in recent decades, to effectively control the practice of pain relief medicine. But a current drama being played out in federal court in Kansas portends an even darker turn in the DOJ's war—a private citizen is being threatened with prosecution for seeking to raise public and news media consciousness of the Feds' war against doctors and patients.

The current contretemps in Wichita has its roots in 2002 when Sean Greenwood, who for more than a decade suffered from a rare but debilitating connective tissue disorder, finally found a remedy. William Hurwitz, a Virginia doctor, prescribed the high doses of pain relief medicine necessary for Greenwood to be able to function day-to-day.

Yet when federal agents raided Hurwitz's clinic in 2003 and charged the pain management specialist with illegal drug trafficking, Greenwood's short-lived return to normalcy ended. He couldn't find another doctor willing to treat his pain—the chances were too good that the "narcs" and the federal prosecutors who work with them would assert impossibly vague federal criminal drug laws. Three years later, Greenwood died from a brain hemorrhage, likely brought on by the blood pressure build-up from years of untreated pain.

Greenwood's wife, Siobhan Reynolds, decided to fight back. In 2003 she founded the Pain Relief Network (PRN), a group of activist, doctors and patients who oppose the federal government's tyranny over pain relief specialists.

Now, the PRN's campaign to raise public awareness of pain-doctor prosecutions has made Reynolds herself the target of drug warriors. Prosecutors in Wichita have asked a federal grand jury to decide whether Reynolds engaged in "obstruction of justice" for her role in seeking to create public awareness, and to otherwise assist the defense, in an ongoing prosecution of Kansas pain relief providers. The feds' message is clear. In the pursuit of pain doctors, private citizen-activists—not just physicians—will be targeted.

For Reynolds, the script of the Kansas prosecution has become all too familiar. The feds announced a 34-count indictment at a December 2007 press conference. Local media dutifully reported the charges with minimal scrutiny and the accused—Dr. Stephen Schneider and his wife, Linda, a nurse—were convicted in the court of public opinion before their trial even began.

In such an atmosphere, it is very difficult to make the point that physicians engaged in the good faith practice of medicine are being second-guessed—not by fellow physicians, but by the federal government—and punished under the criminal law for administering what the Drug Enforcement Agency (DEA) of the Department of Justice considers more narcotics than is necessary to alleviate a patient's pain.

When pain doctors administer too much of a controlled substance, or do so knowing that they will be diverted to narcotic addicts, they are deemed no longer engaged in the legitimate practice of medicine. But the dividing line is far from clear and not subject to universal agreement even within the profession. Any patient in need of relief can, over time, develop a chemical dependence on a lawful drug—much like a diabetic becomes dependent on insulin. And, once a treatment regimen begins, many patients' tolerance to the drug increases. Thus, to produce the same analgesic effect, doctors sometimes need to increase the prescribed amount, and that amount varies from person to person.

It is notoriously difficult even for trained physicians to distinguish an addict's abuse from a patient's dependence. Nonetheless, federal narcotics officers have increasingly terrorized physicians, wielding the criminal law and harsh prison terms to punish perceived violators. Since 2003, over 400 doctors have been criminally prosecuted by the federal government, according to the DEA. One result is that chronic pain patients in this country are routinely undermedicated.

The litany of abusive prosecutorial tactics could fill a volume. A "win-at-all-costs" mentality dominates federal prosecutors and drug agents involved in these cases. After a Miami Beach doctor was acquitted of 141 counts of illegally prescribing pain medication in March 2009, federal district court Judge Alan Gold rebuked the prosecution for introducing government informants—former patients of the doctor who were cooperating to avoid their own prosecution—as impartial witnesses at trial.

Improprieties galore marked the prosecution of Dr. Hurwitz. Before his trial in federal court in Virginia in 2004, the DEA published a "Frequently Asked Questions" (FAQ) pamphlet for prescription pain medications. In a remarkable admission, the DEA wrote that confusion over dependence and addiction "can lead to inappropriate targeting of practitioners and patients for investigation and prosecution." Yet on the eve of the trial, the DEA, realizing that Hurwitz could rely on this government-published pamphlet to defend his treatment methods, withdrew the FAQ from its Web site. Winning the case proved more important than facilitating sound medical practice. Hurwitz was convicted.

In Kansas, it appears that zealous prosecutors are targeting not only the doctors, but also their public advocates. When Reynolds wrote op-eds in local newspapers and granted interviews to other media outlets, Assistant U.S. Attorney Tanya Treadway attempted to impose a gag order on her public advocacy. The district judge correctly denied this extraordinary request.

Undeterred, Treadway filed on March 27 a subpoena demanding a broad range of documents and records, obviously hoping to deter the peripatetic pain relief advocate, or even target her for a criminal trial of her own. Just what was Reynolds' suspected criminal activity?

"Obstruction of justice" is the subpoena's listed offense being investigated, but some of the requested records could, in no possible way, prove such a crime. The prosecutor has demanded copies of an ominous-sounding "movie," which, in reality, is a PRN-produced documentary showing the plight of pain physicians. Also requested were records relating to a billboard Reynolds paid to have erected over a busy Wichita highway. It read: "Dr. Schneider never killed anyone." Suddenly, a rather ordinary exercise in free speech and political activism became evidence of an obstruction of justice.

On Sept. 3, a federal judge will decide whether to enforce this subpoena, which Reynolds' lawyers have sought to invalidate on free speech and other grounds. The citizen's liberty to loudly and publicly oppose the drug warriors' long-running reign of terror on the medical profession and its patients should not be in question. Rather, the question should be how the federal government has managed to accumulate the power to punish doctors who, in good faith, are attempting to alleviate excruciating pain in their patients.

9

Mixing Multiple Medications Causes Health Problems for Elderly Americans

Anne Harding

Anne Harding writes about health-related issues for CNN Health.

Because elderly people take so many medications, they are especially susceptible to problems caused by drug interactions. The more medications a person takes, the more risk there is of overmedication and adverse side effects from the drugs interacting with each other. The problem is compounded because the various specialists that seniors often visit usually do not communicate with each other about new medications or dose changes, and they may prescribe new drugs to treat the side effects caused by other ones. Sedatives and hypnotics are among the riskiest drugs for older people because they increase the likelihood of falls and mental confusion, but nondrug therapies can help reduce the use of such medications. Physicians should regularly review the medications of their older patients to be sure they are taking only what is truly necessary.

Many older adults in the United States are taking a confusing combination of medications, some prescribed by doctors and others picked up over-the-counter or in health food stores.

One in three adults age 57 to 85 is taking at least five prescription drugs, and half regularly use dietary supplements and over-the-counter drugs, according to a study in the *Journal of the American Medical Association*. While any single drug might help people live longer, healthier lives, experts worry that a combination of drugs, along with over-the-counter products and dietary supplements, could be a recipe for disaster in terms of drug interactions.

One in 25 people in the study, or about 2.2 million people, were taking a potentially risky combination of medications. That number jumped to one in 10 among men who were 75 to 85 years old.

For example, some people in the study were taking the blood thinner warfarin along with the cholesterol-lowering drug simvastatin, a combination that can increase the risk of bleeding. Others were taking warfarin and aspirin together, or ginkgo supplements with aspirin, which can also cause problems.

Some Interactions Can Be Fatal

"Half of the interactions we saw increased the risk for bleeding, which could be fatal," said Dima M. Qato of the University of Chicago.

An estimated 175,000 adults 65 and older visit the emergency room every year for treatment of adverse drug events, and about a third of these cases involve commonly used medications.

Dr. Stacy Tessler Lindau of the University of Chicago, who led the research team, points out that the 3,005 study participants were on 15,000 different drugs and supplements in all. She says the percentage of people they identified as being at risk of harmful drug interactions is probably an underestimate given that the researchers only looked at the 20 most commonly used prescription drugs, the 20 most frequently used over-the-counter medications, and the 20 most popular dietary supplements.

"I'm hoping that this study encourages patients and families to be proactive about the medications they're using in terms of getting information from their doctors, their nurses, their pharmacists," says Lindau.

Lindau and her team say that "polypharmacy," or the practice of putting people on multiple drugs, is on the rise. A 2002 study suggested that 23 percent of people 65 and older were on five or more prescription drugs at once, compared with 29 percent in the new study.

Lindau and her team interviewed a nationally representative sample of men and women who were 57 to 85 years old between June 2005 and March 2006. They visited participants in their homes and asked to see containers for every drug or supplement they took regularly.

The number of prescription medications an older person takes is the strongest predictor of their risk for future drug-related problems.

"Literally folks went to their medicine cabinet or kitchen cabinet and brought all of the medications to the table," says Lindau.

Prescription Drug Statistics

Eighty-one percent of the study participants were taking at least one prescription drug, 42 percent were on at least one over-the-counter medication, and 49 percent were using one or more dietary supplement

The most commonly used prescription and over-the-counter drugs were for treating or preventing heart disease, such as cholesterol-lowering statins, blood-pressure-lowering drugs, and blood thinners like warfarin and aspirin.

Polypharmacy was most common among the oldest patients, with 37 percent of men and 36 percent of women 75 to

85 years old taking five or more prescription drugs at once. Women were more likely than men to take prescription drugs and dietary supplements.

The number of prescription medications an older person takes is the strongest predictor of their risk for future drug-related problems, says Dr. Donna Fick, an associate professor of nursing and psychiatry at Pennsylvania State University in University Park.

More Medications, More Problems

"Because we know that the more medications you're on the more problems you have, I think we do have to think harder about how to balance medication use with non-pharmacological approaches," says Fick, a specialist in gerontological nursing.

Sedatives and hypnotics are among the riskiest drugs for older people, increasing the likelihood of falls and mental impairment, she pointed out. They are used to reduce agitation in older adults, but research has shown that offering people warm milk, herbal tea and a back-rub can reduce the use of these medications and the likelihood of drug-induced confusion.

Such approaches are "different than this sort of 'fast food' approach to giving a medication, it takes more time and someone has to reimburse for that," Fick notes. "Right now they don't reimburse you to give back rubs and herbal tea, but they do reimburse you to give a medication, and it's faster."

Another problem, she adds, is that there's currently no way for doctors or pharmacists to know every drug, over-the-counter medication and supplement a patient is taking.

Medication Review

People should try to meet with the same doctor every three to six months to go over all the medications and supplements they are taking, Fick recommends. While it's never a good idea to stop taking a prescribed drug without consulting a doctor, she says, "It's reasonable to say 'Do I need to stay on this?'" And it's also reasonable, she adds, to ask about alternatives to medication.

Lindau also suggests that people try to use the same pharmacy whenever possible, so that the pharmacist can catch potential drug interactions.

"That does help maintain the chain of communication," she says. And when buying an over-the-counter drug or supplement, even cold medicine or vitamins, Lindau recommends purchasing it at the pharmacy counter, which can help remind people to ask about safety.

She also suggests that people keep a list of all the drugs and supplements they're taking in their wallet, and make copies to keep by the telephone and to give to family members and friends who might be contacted in case of an emergency.

Overuse of Antibiotics Creates Drug-Resistant Bacteria

Martha Mendoza and Margie Mason

Martha Mendoza is an Associated Press (AP) writer who has reported from Norway and England. Margie Mason is an AP medical writer based in Vietnam.

The global overuse of antibiotics has caused bacteria to mutate and become resistant to them. One of the most dangerous is MRSA—Methicillin-Resistant Staphylococcus aureus—a *deadly and hard-to-treat "superbug" that has become common in hospitals everywhere. While hospitals around the world struggle to keep MRSA under control, Norway has all but eliminated MRSA infections by simply not prescribing antibiotics to patients unless they are absolutely essential and by isolating those who do have MRSA until they are well. The result is that the number of MRSA cases in Norway has dropped dramatically; in Norway, MRSA now accounts for just 1 percent of all staph infections, while in Japan it accounts for 80 percent and in the United States 63 percent. Other countries—including the United States—are now adopting Norway's conservative attitude about antibiotics in the hope that it will reverse what the World Health Organization calls one of the world's leading public health threats.*

Aker University Hospital is a dingy place to heal. The floors are streaked and scratched. A light layer of dust coats the blood pressure monitors. A faint stench of urine and bleach wafts from a pile of soiled bedsheets dropped in a corner.

Look closer, however, at a microscopic level, and this place is pristine. There is no sign of a dangerous and contagious staph infection that killed tens of thousands of patients in the most sophisticated hospitals of Europe, North America and Asia this year [2009], soaring virtually unchecked.

The reason: Norwegians stopped taking so many drugs.

Twenty-five years ago, Norwegians were also losing their lives to this bacteri[um]. But Norway's public health system fought back with an aggressive program that made it the most infection-free country in the world. A key part of that program was cutting back severely on the use of antibiotics.

Now a spate of new studies from around the world prove that Norway's model can be replicated with extraordinary success, and public health experts are saying these deaths—19,000 in the U.S. each year alone, more than from AIDS—are unnecessary.

The more antibiotics are consumed, the more resistant bacteria develop.

"It's a very sad situation that in some places so many are dying from this, because we have shown here in Norway that Methicillin-resistant Staphylococcus aureus (MRSA) can be controlled, and with not too much effort," said Jan Hendrik-Binder, Oslo's MRSA medical adviser. "But you have to take it seriously, you have to give it attention, and you must not give up."

The World Health Organization says antibiotic resistance is one of the leading public health threats on the planet. A six-month investigation by The Associated Press found overuse and misuse of medicines has led to mutations in once curable diseases like tuberculosis and malaria, making them harder and in some cases impossible to treat.

Now, in Norway's simple solution, there's a glimmer of hope.

How Norway Found the Answer

Dr. John Birger Haug shuffles down Aker's scuffed corridors, patting the pocket of his baggy white scrubs. "My bible," the infectious disease specialist says, pulling out a little red Antibiotic Guide that details this country's impressive MRSA solution.

It's what's missing from this book—an array of antibiotics—that makes it so remarkable.

"There are times I must show these golden rules to our doctors and tell them they cannot prescribe something, but our patients do not suffer more and our nation, as a result, is mostly infection free," he says.

Norway's model is surprisingly straightforward.

- Norwegian doctors prescribe fewer antibiotics than any other country, so people do not have a chance to develop resistance to them.

- Patients with MRSA are isolated and medical staff who test positive stay at home.

- Doctors track each case of MRSA by its individual strain, interviewing patients about where they've been and who they've been with, testing anyone who has been in contact with them.

Haug unlocks the dispensary, a small room lined with boxes of pills, bottles of syrups and tubes of ointment. What's here? Medicines considered obsolete in many developed countries. What's not? Some of the newest, most expensive antibiotics, which aren't even registered for use in Norway, "because if we have them here, doctors will use them," he says.

He points to an antibiotic. "If I treated someone with an infection in Spain with this penicillin I would probably be thrown in jail," he says, "and rightly so because it's useless there."

Countering Coughs and Colds

Norwegians are sanguine about their coughs and colds, toughing it out through low-grade infections.

"We don't throw antibiotics at every person with a fever. We tell them to hang on, wait and see, and we give them a Tylenol to feel better," says Haug.

Convenience stores in downtown Oslo are stocked with an amazing and colorful array—42 different brands at one downtown 7-Eleven—of soothing, but non-medicated, lozenges, sprays and tablets. All workers are paid on days they, or their children, stay home sick. And drug makers aren't allowed to advertise, reducing patient demands for prescription drugs.

In fact, most marketing here sends the opposite message: "Penicillin is not a cough medicine," says the tissue packet on the desk of Norway's MRSA control director, Dr. Petter Elstrom.

He recognizes his country is "unique in the world and best in the world" when it comes to MRSA. Less than 1 percent of health care providers are positive carriers of MRSA staph.

But Elstrom worries about the bacteria slipping in through other countries. Last year almost every diagnosed case in Norway came from someone who had been abroad.

"So far we've managed to contain it, but if we lose this, it will be a huge problem," he said. "To be very depressing about it, we might in some years be in a situation where MRSA is so endemic that we have to stop doing advanced surgeries, things like organ transplants, if we can't prevent infections. In the worst case scenario we are back to 1913, before we had antibiotics."

The Origins of the Problem

Forty years ago, a new spectrum of antibiotics enchanted public health officials, quickly quelling one infection after another. In wealthier countries that could afford them, patients and providers came to depend on antibiotics. Trouble was, the more antibiotics are consumed, the more resistant bacteria develop.

Norway responded swiftly to initial MRSA outbreaks in the 1980s by cutting antibiotic use. Thus while they got ahead of the infection, the rest of the world fell behind.

In Norway, MRSA has accounted for less than 1 percent of staph infections for years. That compares to 80 percent in Japan, the world leader in MRSA; 44 percent in Israel; and 38 percent in Greece.

In the U.S., cases have soared and MRSA cost $6 billion last year [2008]. Rates have gone up from 2 percent in 1974 to 63 percent in 2004. And in the United Kingdom, they rose from about 2 percent in the early 1990s to about 45 percent, although an aggressive control program is now starting to work.

About 1 percent of people in developed countries carry MRSA on their skin. Usually harmless, the bacteria can be deadly when they enter a body, often through a scratch. MRSA spreads rapidly in hospitals where sick people are more vulnerable, but there have been outbreaks in prisons, gyms, even on beaches. When dormant, the bacteria are easily detected by a quick nasal swab and destroyed by antibiotics.

Do the Right Thing

Dr. John Jernigan at the U.S. Centers for Disease Control and Prevention [CDC] said they incorporate some of Norway's solutions in varying degrees, and his agency "requires hospitals to move the needle, to show improvement, and if they don't show improvement they need to do more."

And if they don't?

"Nobody is accountable to our recommendations," he said, "but I assume hospitals and institutions are interested in doing the right thing."

Dr. Barry Farr, a retired epidemiologist who watched a successful MRSA control program launched 30 years ago at the University of Virginia's hospitals, blamed the CDC for clinging to past beliefs that hand washing is the best way to stop the spread of infections like MRSA. He says it's time to add screening and isolation methods to their controls.

The CDC needs to "eat a little crow and say, 'Yeah, it does work,'" he said. "There's example after example. We don't need another study. We need somebody to just do the right thing."

Exporting Norway's Lessons

But can Norway's program really work elsewhere?

The answer lies in the busy laboratory of an aging little public hospital about 100 miles outside of London. It's here that microbiologist Dr. Lynne Liebowitz got tired of seeing the stunningly low Nordic MRSA rates while facing her own burgeoning cases.

So she turned Queen Elizabeth Hospital in Kings Lynn into a petri dish, asking doctors to almost completely stop using two antibiotics known for provoking MRSA infections.

Around the world, various medical providers have . . . successfully adapted Norway's program with encouraging results.

One month later, the results were in: MRSA rates were tumbling. And they've continued to plummet. Five years ago [in 2004], the hospital had 47 MRSA bloodstream infections. This year they've had one.

"I was shocked, shocked," says Liebowitz, bouncing onto her toes and grinning as colleagues nearby drip blood onto slides and peer through microscopes in the hospital laboratory.

When word spread of her success, Liebowitz's phone began to ring. So far she has replicated her experiment at four other hospitals, all with the same dramatic results.

"It's really very upsetting that some patients are dying from infections which could be prevented," she says. "It's wrong."

Around the world, various medical providers have also successfully adapted Norway's program with encouraging results. A medical center in Billings, Mont., cut MRSA infections by 89 percent by increasing screening, isolating patients and making all staff—not just doctors—responsible for increasing hygiene.

In Japan, with its cutting-edge technology and modern hospitals, about 17,000 people die from MRSA every year.

Dr. Satoshi Hori, chief infection control doctor at Juntendo University Hospital in Tokyo, says doctors overprescribe antibiotics because they are given financial incentives to push drugs on patients.

Hori now limits antibiotics only to patients who really need them and screens and isolates high-risk patients. So far his hospital has cut the number of MRSA cases by two-thirds.

VA Hospitals See Success

In 2001, the CDC approached a Veterans Affairs [VA] hospital in Pittsburgh about conducting a small test program. It started in one unit, and within four years, the entire hospital was screening everyone who came through the door for MRSA. The result: an 80 percent decrease in MRSA infections. The program has now been expanded to all 153 VA hospitals, resulting in a 50 percent drop in MRSA bloodstream infections, said Dr. Robert Muder, chief of infectious diseases at the VA Pittsburgh Healthcare System.

"It's kind of a no-brainer," he said. "You save people pain, you save people the work of taking care of them, you save money, you save lives and you can export what you learn to other hospital-acquired infections."

Pittsburgh's program has prompted all other major hospital-acquired infections to plummet as well, saving roughly $1 million a year.

"So, how do you pay for it?" Muder asked. "Well, we just don't pay for MRSA infections, that's all."

A Mother's Crusade

Beth Reimer of Batavia, Ill., became an advocate for MRSA precautions after her 5-week-old daughter Madeline caught a cold that took a fatal turn. One day her beautiful baby had the sniffles. The next?

"She wasn't breathing. She was limp," the mother recalled. "Something was terribly wrong."

MRSA had invaded her little lungs. The antibiotics were useless. Maddie struggled to breathe, swallow, survive, for two weeks.

"For me to sit and watch Madeline pass away from such an aggressive form of something, to watch her fight for her little life—it was too much," Reimer said.

Since Madeline's death, Reimer has become outspoken about the need for better precautions, pushing for methods successfully used in Norway. She's stunned, she said, that anyone disputes the need for change.

"Why are they fighting for this not to take place?" she said.

"Doctor Shopping" Can Lead to Overmedication, Abuse, and Death

Madison Park

Madison Park is a writer and producer for CNN Health.

Michael Jackson, Anna Nicole Smith, Health Ledger, Corey Haim. What all these big-name celebrities have in common—besides dying tragically—is that they are believed to have been "doctor shoppers" who obtained numerous prescriptions for powerful painkillers and sedatives by visiting a variety of different physicians under false pretenses. The abuse of prescription medications is a growing problem, and doctor shopping is one of the primary ways that prescription pill addicts get their drugs. Most states do not require physicians to check a patient's drug history, and doctors say it can be very difficult to tell who comes to them with a legitimate need and who just wants to obtain drugs. Prescription monitoring programs and increased drug abuse screening in clinics and doctor's offices are two ways to combat this problem.

Former child actor Corey Haim had prescriptions for as many as 553 dangerous drugs in the last year of his life, and it's the result of "doctor shopping," California's top law official said [in April 2010].

The issue of doctor shopping—visiting numerous doctors to fraudulently get prescription drugs—has been raised in numerous celebrity deaths, including Anna Nicole Smith, Michael Jackson and Heath Ledger. Doctors say they often rely on their own instant judgments in the office and have little reliable means of double-checking the patients' information.

"It puts doctors in the uncomfortable position of playing private eye," said Dr. Lance Longo, medical director of Addiction Psychiatry at Aurora Behavioral Health Services in Milwaukee, Wisconsin. "We're trained to relieve pain and suffering. Unfortunately, with the widespread misuse of controlled substances and diversion risks, we're often taken advantage of."

Haim obtained doses of Vicodin, Valium, Soma, Oxycontin and Xanax from seven doctors, filled at seven pharmacies, said California Attorney General Jerry Brown in a news conference [in April 2010]. Vicodin and Oxycontin are painkillers; Valium and Xanax are anti-anxiety medications; Soma is a muscle relaxant.

The 38-year-old actor died last month [March 2010] after collapsing at a Los Angeles apartment. . . .

Haim had visited several emergency rooms and urgent care clinics with complaints of an injured shoulder or depression, according to investigators.

Doctor Shoppers Dupe Doctors

Doctor shoppers often visit facilities where medical professionals don't know them, experts say. They also call during weekends or ask for prescription refills using excuses such as having dropped the pills in toilets or getting pills wet on a camping trip, physicians said.

Misuse of prescription drugs is a growing problem. Estimated hospitalizations for poisoning by prescription opioids, sedatives and tranquilizers increased 65 percent from 1999 to 2006, according to a study in the May [2010] edition of the *American Journal of Preventive Medicine*.

Doctor shopping is a problem, but it's not the chief way prescription drugs end up with people for whom they're not intended, said David Brushwood, professor of pharmaceutical outcomes and policy at the University of Florida in Gainesville.

"It's a relatively insignificant source of diverted prescription drugs, as compared with theft from drug stores, warehouses, acquisition over the Internet, theft from people's homes."

To curb prescription drug abuse, 34 states have prescription monitoring programs, but their requirements and effectiveness vary, experts said.

In those states, a record from the prescription drug purchase is sent to the state agency that oversees the monitoring programs. Doctors can request reports online and find out what medications a patient has received in the past six months to a year.

This information helps doctors, said John Eadie, director of the Prescription Drug Monitoring Program Center of Excellence at Brandeis University.

"There are doctor shoppers, who see 15 doctors and pharmacies or more by deceiving physicians for professed pain and other disability that would cause prescribing these drugs," he said. "If doctors know they are obtaining drugs from other prescribers, they might be really reluctant to prescribe."

But these monitoring programs have limitations, Brushwood said.

It's easy to dodge the system by providing different names and identification numbers or buying drugs in neighboring states, he said. Most state laws do not require the doctors to look at the patient's drug history.

Many health professionals don't use the monitoring system anyway, Brushwood said. In his research, many expressed skepticism about the accuracy of the information and complained it was "time consuming" and did not "seem necessary," he said.

Screening Can Identify Likely Addicts

Doctors have other tools to prevent being duped.

"We're doing addiction screening in our clinics," said Dr. Doris K. Cope, professor and vice chairman for pain medicine in the department of anesthesiology at the University of Pittsburgh School of Medicine. "If someone is at high risk for addiction, we try to identify them, and we have one of our pain psychologists evaluate them. We then make appropriate referrals for their continued care."

> *"This is the addiction epidemic of our time."*

They also test urine to see whether it matches the patient's medication history.

"If someone comes in and can barely move, they put on this big drama, then you see them get up and run out the door, even my youngest son could figure that out," said Cope, a member of the American Society of Anesthesiologists' Committee on Pain Medicines.

Some employ clever strategies such as memorizing symptoms to get a certain prescription or telling their doctors they have allergies to particular medication to get a stronger drug. But physicians have to walk a fine line, said Longo, a psychiatrist.

"We all have the expectation to practice prudent, conscientious medicine, but we're not trained to be DEA [Drug Enforcement Administration] agents," Longo said. "We don't want to alienate patients who aren't addicted or abusing drugs. The majority of patients who have legitimate illnesses feel stigmatized getting controlled drugs."

Some of the popularly abused drugs include oxycodone, hydrocodone, benzodiazepine and methamphetamine.

"This is the addiction epidemic of our time," Longo said.

Organizations to Contact

The editors have compiled the following list of organizations concerned with the issues debated in this book. The descriptions are derived from materials provided by the organizations. All have publications or information available for interested readers. The list was compiled on the date of publication of the present volume; the information provided here may change. Readers need to remember that many organizations take several weeks or longer to respond to inquiries.

Alliance for the Prudent Use of Antibiotics (APUA)
5 Kneeland St., Boston, MA   02111
(617) 636-0966 • fax: (617) 636-3999
e-mail: apua@tufts.edu
website: www.tufts.edu/med/apua

Alliance for the Prudent Use of Antibiotics's mission is to strengthen society's defenses against infectious disease by promoting appropriate antimicrobial access and use, and by controlling antimicrobial resistance on a worldwide basis. Its website offers extensive information for consumers and doctors about the proper use of antibiotics and the danger that their overuse will lead to their ineffectiveness.

Center for Drug Evaluation and Research
Food and Drug Administration, Silver Spring, MD   20993
(301) 796-3400
e-mail: druginfo@fda.hhs.gov
website: www.fda.gov/cder

The Center for Drug Evaluation and Research promotes and protects the health of Americans by assuring that prescription and over-the-counter drugs are safe and effective. The center routinely monitors TV, radio, and print advertisements to see that they are truthful and balanced. It publishes the *News Along the Pike* newsletter as well as various reports.

Center for Public Integrity

910 Seventeenth St. NW, Ste. 700, Washington, DC 20006
(202) 466-1300
website: www.publicintegrity.org/rx

The Center for Public Integrity is a nonprofit, nonpartisan, nonadvocacy, independent journalism organization. Its mission is to produce original investigative journalism about significant public issues to make institutional power more transparent and accountable. It conducts a project titled Pushing Prescriptions: How the Drug Industry Sells Its Agenda at Your Expense, which has a website with extensive information about the political influence of the pharmaceutical industry.

Children and Adults Against Drugging America (CHAADA)

e-mail: info@chaada.org
website: www.chaada.org

Children and Adults Against Drugging America is a membership organization whose goal is to raise awareness about what it perceives as the overmedicating of America and the deception occurring within the psychiatric profession—which it views as preying on innocent people, especially children, in order to turn a profit—and the dangers of the drugs used to treat alleged mental illnesses. The organization opposes the use of all psychotropic drugs. Its website contains extensive material about personal experiences with the adverse effects of drugs and about drug-related legislation.

International Coalition for Drug Awareness

website: www.drugawareness.org

This organization is a private nonprofit group of physicians, researchers, journalists, and concerned citizens focused on "the world's most pervasive and subtle drug problem—prescription drugs." Available at its website is the full-length film *Prescription for Disaster*, an in-depth investigation into the symbiotic relationships between the pharmaceutical industry, the FDA, lobbyists, lawmakers, medical schools, and researchers. The site also includes material about individuals' negative experiences with prescription drugs and links to many sites about specific drug dangers.

International Federation of Pharmaceutical Manufacturers and Associations (IFPMA)

15 Chemin Louis-Dunant, Geneva 20   1211
  Switzerland
e-mail: admin@ifpma.org
website: www.ifpma.org

International Federation of Pharmaceutical Manufacturers and Associations is a nonprofit, nongovernmental organization representing pharmaceutical industry associations from both developed and developing countries. It aims to encourage a global policy environment that is conducive to innovation in medicine, both therapeutic and preventive, for the benefit of patients around the world. Its website contains information about its position on issues such as improving access to health care, the ethical promotion of drugs, and the problem of counterfeit medicines.

National Council on Patient Information and Education (NCPIE)

200-A Monroe St., Ste. 212, Rockville, MD   20850-4448
(301) 340-3940 • fax: (301) 340-3944
e-mail: ncpie@ncpie.info
website: www.talkaboutrx.org

National Council on Patient Information and Education is a coalition of over 125 diverse organizations whose mission is to stimulate and improve communication of information on appropriate medicine use to consumers and health-care professionals. NCPIE publishes educational resources, including *Make Notes & Take Notes to Avoid Medication Errors*. Its website contains a section designed to help caregivers and patients become well-informed medicine users who know where to go for reliable information, and what questions to ask.

National Pharmaceutical Council (NPC)

1894 Preston White Dr., Reston, VA   20191
(703) 620-6390 • fax: (703) 476-0904
website: http://npcnow.org

Supported by more than twenty of the nation's major research-based pharmaceutical companies, National Pharmaceutical Council sponsors research and education projects aimed at demonstrating the appropriate use of medicines to improve health outcomes. It focuses on the use of evidence-based medicine to help patients make the best, most cost-effective health-care decisions. Monographs on disease management, newsletters, and other publications geared to policy makers, healthcare providers, employers, and consumers are available on its website.

No Free Lunch

e-mail: contact@nofreelunch.org
website: www.nofreelunch.org

No Free Lunch is a nonprofit organization of health-care providers and medical students who believe that pharmaceutical promotion should not guide clinical practice. Its website has slide presentations on the relationship between physicians and the pharmaceutical industry as well as information for patients, including a directory of doctors who have pledged not to accept gifts from drug companies.

Pharmaceutical Research and Manufacturers of America (PhRMA)

950 F St. NW, Ste. 300, Washington, DC   20004
(202) 835-3400 • fax: (202) 835-3414
website: www.phrma.org

Pharmaceutical Research and Manufacturers of America represents US drug research and biotechnology companies. It advocates public policies that encourage discovery of important medicines, and its medical officers sometimes testify before

Congress on issues such as drug advertising, safety, and importation. Among its publications is *PhRMA Guiding Principles: Direct to Consumer Advertisements About Prescription Medicines.*

PharmedOut

Georgetown University, Washington, DC   20057
(202) 687-1191 • fax: (202) 687-7407
website: www.pharmedout.org

PharmedOut is an independent, publicly funded project that empowers physicians to identify and counter inappropriate pharmaceutical promotion practices. Its website offers many links to YouTube videos, articles, and Web resources that are of interest to consumers as well as doctors.

Worst Pills, Best Pills

Public Citizen, Washington, DC   20009
website: www.worstpills.org

Worstpills.org is researched, written, and maintained by Public Citizen's Health Research Group, a division of Public Citizen, which is a nonprofit, nonpartisan public-interest group that represents consumer interests in federal government at all levels: Congress, the executive branch, and the courts. Although most of its information about specific drugs is accessible only to subscribers, its website contains a number of free consumer guides, including "Misprescribing and Overprescribing of Drugs," and "Drugs, Money and Politics," among others.

Bibliography

Books

John Abramson	*Overdosed America: The Broken Promise of American Medicine.* New York: HarperPerennial, 2008.
Marcia Angell	*The Truth About the Drug Companies.* New York: Random House, 2005.
Peter R. Breggin and Dick Scruggs	*Talking Back to Ritalin: What Doctors Aren't Telling You About Stimulants and ADHD.* Rev. ed. Cambridge, MA: Da Capo Press, 2001.
Greg Critser	*Generation Rx: How Prescription Drugs Are Altering American Lives, Minds, and Bodies.* Boston: Houghton Mifflin Harcourt, 2005.
Lawrence Diller	*Running on Ritalin: A Physician Reflects on Children, Society, and Performance in a Pill.* New York: Bantam, 1999.
Ray Moynihan and Alan Cassels	*Selling Sickness: How the World's Biggest Pharmaceutical Companies Are Turning Us All into Patients.* New York: Nation Books, 2006.
Ray Strand and Donna K. Wallace	*Death by Prescription: The Shocking Truth Behind an Overmedicated Nation.* Nashville: Thomas Nelson, 2003.

Judith Warner — *We've Got Issues: Children and Parents in the Age of Medication.* New York: Riverhead Books, 2010.

Ethan Watters — *Crazy Like Us: The Globalization of the American Psyche.* Glencoe, IL: Free Press, 2010.

Marilyn Webb — *The Good Death: The New American Search to Reshape the End of Life.* New York: Bantam, 1999.

Periodicals

Alliance for the Prudent Use of Antibiotics — "Shadow Epidemic: The Growing Menace of Drug Resistance," Executive Summary of the 2005 GAARD Report. Boston: APUA, 2005.

Karen O. Anderson et al. — "Racial and Ethnic Disparities in Pain: Causes and Consequences of Unequal Care," *Journal of Pain*, December 2009.

Associated Press — "Haim Got Pills Via 'Doctor Shopping'—Actor Reportedly Got 553 in His Final Two Months," *San Diego Union Tribune*, April 7, 2010.

Douglas J. Edwards — "Report Raises Concerns About Overmedicating Seniors," *NH News Notes: Nursing Homes*, August 2003.

Judy Holland   "Are Kids Being Overmedicated?—Psychiatrists Say Schools Steer Parents to Overmedicate Kids," *New York Times*, October 2, 2000.

Gregory M. Lamb   "Why Are We Taking So Many Pills? Marketers Have Convinced Many That There's a Drug for Everything," *Christian Science Monitor*, October 25, 2005.

Elizabeth Large   "Americans Are Taking More Prescription Drugs than Ever Before, Raising the Question: Are We an Overmedicated Society?" *Baltimore Sun*, December 17, 2004.

Jonah Lehrer   "Depression's Upside," *New York Times Magazine*, February 25, 2010.

Catherine Lewis   "Why Is Your Doctor Getting Your Child Hooked on Unnecessary Drugs?" *Insiders Health*, November 9, 2009.

Rick Mayes and Jennifer Erkulwater   "Medicating Kids: Pediatric Mental Health Policy and the Tipping Point for ADHD and Stimulants," *Journal of Policy History*, vol. 20, no. 3, 2008.

Elizabeth J. Roberts   "A Rush to Medicate Young Minds," *Washington Post*, October 8, 2006.

Vera Sharav   "America's Overmedicated Children," *Youth and Medicines*, June 1, 2005.

Maia Szalavitz   "Let a Thousand Licensed Poppies
                  Bloom," *New York Times*, July 13,
                  2005.

Time   "Are We Giving Kids Too Many
                  Drugs?" November 3, 2003.

Barry Yeoman   "Prisoners of Pain—Why Are
                  Millions of Suffering Americans
                  Being Denied the Prescription Drug
                  Relief They Need?" *AARP Magazine*,
                  September & October 2005.

Index